The Rainbow Bridge

Praise for *The Rainbow Bridge*:

'An original, interestingly-imagined and challenging book.
Its finely-textured writing with historical flavour and a
strong plot make this a rare achievement.'
The Irish Times

'Flegg is one of the finest writers of children's literature in Ireland
today. Many passages in this novel are a pure pleasure to read.'
Inis

Praise for *Wings Over Delft*, Book 1 in the *Louise* trilogy:

'A remarkably engaging story, in which themes of love, art and history
are powerfully combined. The unfolding narrative is dramatic, passionate
and brilliantly set. The quality of the writing throughout is superb and
the ending unforgettably moving.'
Robert Dunbar, critic and broadcaster

'The gentle love story takes the reader through dark intrigue, religious
unrest and the palpable, cultural atmosphere of life in a Dutch city, to
an unexpected conclusion. A well-tailored and absorbing read for
adults as well as for age 12-plus.'
The Sunday Tribune

'Flegg gives us an exquisitely crafted novel which will stay in the reader's
memory long after the closing pages are read. The ending is unexpected
and dramatic and leaves the reader eagerly awaiting the subsequent
books in the Louise trilogy.'
Valerie Coghlan, Inis

AUBREY FLEGG was born in Dublin and spent his early childhood on a farm in County Sligo. His later schooldays were spent in England, but he returned to Dublin to study geology. After a period of research in Kenya he joined the Geological Survey of Ireland; he is now retired and lives in Dublin with his wife, Jennifer.

Aubrey's first book, *Katie's War*, won the IBBY Sweden Peter Pan Award 2000. It was followed by *The Cinnamon Tree*, the story of an African girl who steps on a landmine. *Wings Over Delft*, the first book in the *Louise* trilogy, won the Bisto Book of the Year Award 2004, Ireland's most prestigious children's literature prize, and is included in the White Ravens 2004 collection – a selection of outstanding international books for children and young adults made by the International Youth Library in Munich. In 2005 it won the Reading Association of Ireland Award. The *Louise* trilogy will be completed by *In the Claws of the Eagle*. Aubrey's books have been translated into German, Swedish, Danish, Serbian and Slovene.

The Rainbow Bridge

*Book 2: the **Louise** trilogy*

Aubrey Flegg

THE O'BRIEN PRESS
DUBLIN

First published 2004 by The O'Brien Press Ltd,
20 Victoria Road, Dublin 6, Ireland.
Tel. +353 1 4923333; Fax. +353 1 4922777
E-mail: books@obrien.ie
Website: www.obrien.ie
This edition published 2006

ISBN-10: 0-86278-917-6
ISBN-13: 978-0-86278-917-6

British Library Cataloguing-in-Publication Data
Flegg, Aubrey M.
The rainbow bridge. - (The Louise trilogy ; bk. 2)
1.Portraits - Fiction 2.Hussars - Fiction
3.France - History - 1789-1900 - Fiction 4.Young adult fiction
I.Title
823.9'14[J]

2 3 4 5 6 7
06 07 08 09 10

The O'Brien Press receives
assistance from

Typesetting, editing, layout and design: The O'Brien Press Ltd
Cover artwork by Henriette Sauvant, ©, courtesy of C. Bertelsmann Kinder- und
Jugendbuchverlag, a division of Verlagsgruppe Random House, Germany
Printing: Nørhaven Paperback A/S
Author photograph: Jennifer Flegg

The *Louise* trilogy is dedicated
to Bill Darlison

Even the rainbow has a body

made of the drizzling rain

and is an architecture of glistening atoms

built up, built up

yet you can't lay your hand on it,

nay, nor even your mind.

'The Rainbow', *D H Lawrence*.

The Rainbow Bridge is dedicated to
Jennifer

ACKNOWLEDGEMENTS

I am deeply indebted to my family and to my friends for their help, advice and support during the writing of *The Rainbow Bridge*, not all of whom can be listed here. My love and gratitude to Jennifer, my wife, who has picked me up and dusted me down when I have tried to climb on rainbows. To Patrick and Margaret Kelly who, with Jan de Fouw, read my early draft and have shared with me their knowledge and wisdom, my grateful thanks. Any errors that may have crept in are of my making. A special word of thanks to Louise Fitzpatrick, and to my younger reader, Sam Fitzpatrick (no relation), who between them gave me warning when my last chapters were going astray. My thanks to Nicolas Canal whose spirited singing of '*The Marseillaise*' convinced me that that song alone could quell any mob.

Then there are my thanks to all at The O'Brien Press who have provided me with cheerful encouragement throughout. My personal debt to Michael O'Brien is but a reflection of the debt owed to him by everyone involved in children's literature in Ireland. Thanks also to Íde ní Laoghaire, and to all of the production team, particularly Emma Byrne for her cover design. Now a very special word of thanks to Mary Webb, my editor: thank you Mary, they never said it was going to be easy, but you kept with me every step of the way with your attention to detail, encouragement and ideas.

Finally my thanks to Bill Darlison for our many discussions, agreements, and to a lesser extent, disagreements. From Bill I have learned that living with questions is sometimes better than living with answers.

CONTENTS

On 12 October 1654 at half past ten in the morning, Willie Claes, the watchman at Delft's gunpowder store, absentmindedly placed a still-burning tobacco pipe in his pocket before he returned to his duties. Minutes later, an explosion took place that tore the heart out of the small Dutch town; it levelled over two hundred houses, and wiped out whole families in the process. Among the dead was sixteen-year-old Louise Eeden. The only record of her was her newly painted portrait, which survived, knocked askew on its easel in the studio of Master Jacob Haitink. Over a century would pass before the Master's picture would be rediscovered and Louise would begin once again to affect the lives of others.

CHAPTER 1

France 1792

Gaston Morteau

'Ta, ta, taaa ta, Taaa ta, ta ...? *Ah zut!* I so nearly have it. That tune has been in my head all night ... Is there more coffee?' Gaston hardly noticed as Colette got up quietly and refilled his cup for him. They were sitting at breakfast in the cavernous kitchen of the old winery, grouped about the end of the long table that could seat twenty or more vineyard workers when the season demanded it. The elegant rooms in the front of the house, which faced onto the street, were seldom used. Gaston abandoned his musical efforts and leaned back comfortably in his chair. He looked benignly around the table, consciously absorbing the details of the room and the company, as someone does who is about to leave home. Facing him was his father, chief winemaker – *vigneron* – to the Count du Bois who owned the vineyards that lined the gentle valley in which their village nestled. Even the village name reflected its history: Les Clos du Bois, the vineyards of the Count du Bois. His mother was sitting at the head of the table, straight-backed, looking every bit the aristocrat, which, by birth, she was.

Gaston wondered anew at the contrast between his parents. Papa's face was deeply lined, his skin burned to mahogany from long exposure to wind and sun, making him look older than his forty-five years, but his eyes sparked bright from within the mesh of wrinkles. At the moment he was quietly crumbling the bread beside his plate, his mind far away, probably fondling the grapes that were now swelling to their vintage ripeness under the August sun. He would hold long conversations with his vines, addressing the grapes as if they were a recalcitrant class in school and he their teacher, but he was no fool. The vineyards were his life; when he drank he was like an artist standing back from his work so that he could view it as a whole. As he rolled the wine about on his tongue, his eyes would be seeing the slopes and grapes from which its various flavours sprang, and his ears would be listening to whispered histories of sun and soil, of sudden rain, and deep fermentation. He would hear confessions too: grapes picked too soon – a musty cask – the follies of youth, and like a benign priest, would admonish, and very occasionally, condemn.

For all that he was a dreamer, it was he who, years before, had surprised everyone by carrying off the Count's beautiful cousin to be his wife. And it was to him that the villagers came to relieve themselves of their personal burdens. If they needed straight advice they went to Monsieur Brouchard, the miller, but if they wanted a sympathetic ear they would slip in through the winery gates and seek out Monsieur Morteau among the vines or in the cellars. Gaston would see them deep in conversation and would know to keep away. Between them, Papa Morteau and M. Brouchard knew about most of what went on in and around the village.

Gaston tried to take it all in: his family, his home. Today he would leave them, perhaps never to return, and he must preserve this memory. He was eighteen and it was high time that he went, before the soil caught him and rooted him forever. A soldier's life would be far more exciting. *'Officer*

Cadet Gaston Morteau!' he smiled, imagining himself in the magnificent uniform that was waiting for him upstairs in his bedroom. In it he would be transformed, rising like a phoenix from the ashes of his former self. And he would be fighting for the noblest cause: the defence of his country.

It had been three years since the storming of the Bastille in Paris, when the people had turned against the King and the aristocracy, and begun the Revolution that had swept through France. Castles were burned, noble families were attacked and many emigrated in fear. The arguments for and against the Revolution had swept back and forth around the Morteau table, as in most homes throughout France, with Madame defending the 'noble privileges' and the order imposed by the aristocracy, while Gaston would defend the rights of the people. However, in truth, the village was too out of the way for the turmoil to have had any real effect on them so far.

But now it was different; the Prussians had crossed the border, determined to restore the King to the throne. Gaston's beloved France was under attack, and today he would set off to join the Hussars of Auxerre in their fight against the enemy. As he thought about what might be ahead of him, he wanted to spread his arms and embrace this dear place, his home, and his family.

And so it happened that, still smiling, he looked up and found himself staring into the eyes of Colette. She saw his smile, half returned it, and then dropped her eyes. Gaston felt a stab of guilt. Though the girl had been in the house for nearly six months, he'd hardly noticed her; she was only fourteen, four years younger than he. The poor child's father had been killed just three years ago in Paris in '89, at the very beginning of the Revolution. Hearsay had it that her father had intervened – as he would have done to help anyone in distress – when two elderly aristocrats had been pulled from their coach by the mob. No one knew precisely what had followed. The bodies of all three were found later, and there were no reliable witnesses. Then, last March, the girl's mother, who had been a particular friend of Madame Morteau, had died, and Colette de Valenod was quietly absorbed into their family. It was a tricky time; some of Colette's relatives were under sentence for their royalist sympathies, so the aristocratic 'de' was dropped from her name. For some months Madame had kept her virtually under house arrest, now it was put abroad that she was a distant cousin of the Morteau family.

Colette was staring straight ahead now, her wrists resting dutifully on the edge of the table, head slightly forward so that her dark hair hung loose, part-curtaining her face. She looked lost and vulnerable, the half-smile gone, replaced by the sadness that was her customary demeanour. Gaston's newfound gallantry obliged him to try to restore that smile. This was a day when he wanted everyone to be happy. As if she felt the intensity of his look, hot colour suddenly washed across Colette's face. Gaston picked up his coffee and blew on the surface to cool it.

'Ta, ta, taaa...' he began again.

Colette's head lifted.

'It is rude to sing at table,' his mother interrupted him. 'And I don't think much of the words either.' But behind the criticism there was a glimmer of a smile.

'Oh, I know the words, Maman. I have them by heart; it's just the tune I can't get. I heard it when I went to be fitted for my uniform in Auxerre. It was brought to Paris by a battalion of volunteers from Marseilles, so they call it the 'Marseillaise'.

You will love it – all about country, and patriots, and blood.'
'Blood?' his mother snapped. 'Why does it always have to
be blood? And the poor King, what will happen to him in
prison, and Marie Antoinette … and the boy?'
'They are safer where they are, Mother.'
'No! I don't trust those Girondins, what they really want is
to do away with the monarchy and have a republic instead.
And why did they have to massacre the King's Guard? In
their lovely uniforms!' For all that Mother had married a
commoner she was still an aristocrat and a Royalist at heart.
She and Gaston would spar together as a matter of routine.
'What was it all for?' she asked.

'Mother, the King was in league with our enemies; it's not
just the Prussians, half the countries of Europe are lining up
to put him back on the throne and put the nobles back in
their castles. Do you know what the Duke of Brunswick, the
general who is leading the invasion, says? He says that when
he liberates the King he'll execute the entire population of
Paris? That's blood for you.'

'Well, what have *you* to offer that is better than the nobility?' she challenged.

'Liberty, equality, and fraternity – "*The Rights of Man!*"'

'They have just copied those from the Americans,'
Madame Morteau sniffed. 'We should never have supported
them against the British in '78; you won't remember it, you
were just four, but I do. Now look at the monster it has
unleashed, and on our own soil.'

'But it needn't be a monster, Mother. '*The Rights of Man'* is
our constitution – that all men are born free and equal! We
should know these rights by heart: Liberty, Property, Safety,
and Resistance to Oppression. Sovereignty lies in the nation,
whether we have a king or not. Don't you see that we are

changing the face of Europe? France will stand out as a beacon of hope!'

It was familiar territory to them all. Every once in a while Gaston and his mother had to go through this ritual combat. Even though Father never joined in, Gaston had the uncomfortable feeling that he had a clearer view of the situation than had either of them.

'I don't see anything noble in the common man when he becomes a mob,' Madame Morteau said, tight-lipped. 'Half-crazed, uneducated masses striking down innocent people.'

'That's why we need an *army*, Mother – *disciplined soldiers*.' Gaston, impressed by his own rhetoric, put his hand to his chest. Here he was, setting out to take up arms for his country, to lay down his life for these people: Mother, Father, Colette, the people of the village ...

His fine thoughts were cut short by his mother. 'Have you forgotten that the Count is coming today?' she asked.

Gaston removed his hand. The Count du Bois usually made an appearance in the village on church holidays, and used these occasions to call at the winery and discuss business with Gaston's father.

'He wants to see you in your uniform before you go.'

'My dress-uniform?'

'Of course, what else?'

'Mon Dieu, Maman ... I don't even know how to put it on!'

'I don't think he'll be critical. He didn't pay for it,' Madame Morteau said acidly. The Count, though noted for charm, was notoriously careful of his purse. 'Don't worry, he will feel that his letter of recommendation to your colonel deserves your homage.' While Mother would defend the aristocracy in principle, she gave no quarter when it came to the faults of individual aristocrats, her cousin in particular.

'Will you tell him that you want to buy out that portion of the vineyard that is due to you?' Gaston asked, changing the subject. When his mother had married, part of her marriage settlement had been the right to buy a significant portion of the vineyard from the Count, if she so wished. Papa, however, had steadfastly refused to countenance this. His family had managed the vineyards for the Chateau du Bois for generations; he was an artist and a craftsman, not a landowner. As the Count's vigneron he had the virtual management of the whole valley. The vineyards were his palette, and the wines he created were his pictures. The idea of carving the vineyard up, even to his own advantage, was abhorrent to him. He needed the full palette of colours to create the richness and variety of his wines.

Gaston could see his father shifting uncomfortably in his chair. He felt bad about raising the matter, but with all that was going on in France at the moment, there were no guarantees that the Count would be left in possession of his vineyards. What would happen to Mother's entitlement if the Count fled, or had his land confiscated? If there were no chateau vineyard, who would employ them?

'You know your father doesn't want that,' his mother said with resignation. On matters of principle Father could be immovable. He was getting to his feet now, brushing the crumbs from his shirt.

'No, Gaston. The vineyard is a living thing; it cannot be divided. Each vine, each slope, each acre plays its part in every barrel we produce. I will not destroy what it has taken generations to make as one. The Count has declared for the Republic, he supports the Revolution, and nobody in the village will make any trouble. Our roots are with the chateau.'

Colette helped to clear the table when the meal was over and then joined Margot, the kitchen maid, in the scullery to dry the breakfast cups. She needed to do something practical with her hands. She had been acutely aware of Gaston's stare at breakfast. It felt as if she had walked on to thin ice and felt it cracking beneath her; she found the experience both disturbing and exciting. She wanted to be happy, but whenever she responded to Margot's light-hearted banter she could feel Madame's disapproval, reminding her that she was still in mourning. There was a lot about this family that Colette didn't understand. At one minute she would represent a welcome pair of hands in a busy household, but in the next she would feel that she was being preserved as some sort of relic of her poor mother. What she needed now was the practical clatter of plates, and to hear the latest round in Margot's bid for the heart of Lucien, a worker at the flourmill down by the river. Margot was almost her only contact with the village; Madame kept her so secluded – for her own safety – that she had met hardly anyone outside of the winery. She hurried into the scullery where she found Margot simmering with indignation like a saucepan about to blow its lid.

'Oh, Mademoiselle! You have come at last. I am ready to explode.' Margot opened her eyes to a startling extent. 'Wait till I tell you. Lucien, *le cochon* ... the pig... he swore to me that Bernadette meant nothing to him.' Bernadette was Margot's rival in the battle for Lucien. 'The cow ... she is a slut! Yesterday as I approached the mill I saw someone coming out. "Who is this coming towards me?" I ask myself.' Margot was shortsighted. 'My heart beats faster. Oh! No need to worry … it is just la Bernadette, "Pah!" I say to myself. I raise my nose in the air until she is past.' Margot imitated her own nonchalant walk. 'This woman, she means nothing to Lucien therefore she means nothing to me. I wait till she's past, then I turn to her back and I put my tongue out like this. Ohhhhhh la la, Mademoiselle what did I see?' Margot grabbed Colette's arm with a sudsy hand. 'No wonder she looked like a cat with cream … *merde!*'

'Go on!' said Colette breathlessly. Margot was staring out of the window, her teeth bared. Colette felt another hand close on her elbow from behind but she couldn't turn, she had to hear. 'What did you see, Margot?'

'Oh, Mam'selle, there they were: two hands printed in flour like two white gloves on her back. You should have heard what I–' But Colette was not to hear Margot's denunciation of Bernadette – or was it the luckless Lucien? The hand on her elbow had suddenly become a band of steel as Madame Morteau drew Colette bodily out of the scullery door.

'Come, my dear,' she said severely. 'Leave the dishes to Margot.'

'But Madame, I like to help. Also I like to hear Margot's talk about the village. She–'

'Hush, my dear.' Madame Morteau stopped her. Then, in a softer tone … 'ah, your poor mother, I grieve so much for her. For her sake I mustn't let you become a servant here. This is your home now.' Madame dropped her voice further. 'Margot is a good girl, but you must realise that she is a peasant. I cannot have her filling your ears with village gossip. Also there is the way she speaks … What if your mother were to come back and hear you talking like a girl from the fields?'

Madame Morteau hadn't meant to hurt – she seldom did –

but her choice of words was unfortunate. Colette had held her mother in her arms as she died; she knew there was no coming back from where her mother had gone. Suddenly all her frustration and anger welled up inside her. Tears and helpless rage surged through her. What did her precious aristocratic upbringing matter if it meant she couldn't have friends of her own? She tore her arm from Madame Morteau's grip and ran towards the stairs. At the bottom step she whipped around, Margot's choicest vulgarities seething in her mouth. She tried to get them out, but they choked her. Oh, why couldn't she rage and fume and throw things like other girls? Madame Morteau was looking at her in amazement. Didn't she realise what she had said? Was she stupid? Had she no notion of what it was like to have your family torn away from you? Colette bit hard on her lip; if only she could have her mother back everything would be all right. She threw herself at the stairs and pounded as hard as she could up to the first landing, where she paused, feeling the sharp taste of blood in her mouth.

As she climbed wearily up the next flight, she thought bitterly of how her father had died, trying to save the lives of people who probably meant nothing to him, at the hands of a mob that had good cause to hate him and his class. And then there was Mother, who had starved herself into ill health, because she had been too proud to confess – until it was too late – that she had no money. What use were these old values? And now here *she* was, being preserved like one of those pale and pathetic pressed flowers that fall out of old books.

She reached the top landing and paused to look out of the open window. The road fell away below the house to where the statue of St Vincent stood alone in the village square.

Sparrows were chattering in the eaves above her head. She could hear Gaston humming to himself as he moved about his room to her left. He would be packing for his departure now. If only she could go with him, just to be there and to participate in his adventures. Anything to escape from this dreadful limbo.

'Got it!' Gaston gave a small cry of triumph; had he remembered his tune? He was humming it again. She listened. His confidence was increasing: 'Ta, ta, taaa ta, Taaa …' his voice was gaining strength. Oh to be a man, for whom things were always simple and straightforward, and to be brave without thinking.

Ever since her father's death, Colette had been haunted by fear, her sleep broken by the same nightmare. She had never seen or heard a real mob, but still *the mob* lay in wait each night. She would try to open her eyes but daren't, because she knew that their faces would be there, pressed up close, terrifying, screaming, distorted faces full of hate for Father and her. Then, in a sudden silence, the killing would start. Grunts, and the sound of blows falling again and again on her father. She knew she could stop the murder if she only could wake in time, but she never could. And so each night was approached in terror and each day began with a feeling of having failed him.

She walked down the short corridor to her room where she lay down on her coverlet and stared at the cracks on the ceiling. Gaston would be gone soon, just when he seemed to have finally noticed her.

Colette woke with a start. The sun had moved while she slept. She felt refreshed and was surprised to find her face stiff from tears. She poured the remains of the water from her jug into a basin and washed her face. Then, taking the jug with her, she hurried for the stairs. It would soon be time to start preparing for dinner. Madame would have forgotten this morning's incident. Perhaps she'd be able to corner Margot and hear the rest of the Lucien saga. First, however, she'd tap on Gaston's door and ask if he needed water too. Her knock produced an immediate response.

'Is that Colette? Come at once, you must help me!' It was an order. This would be what it would be like to be a soldier under his command, she thought.

'What's the matter?'

'I'm in trouble. I'm quite respectable ... I think.' She put down her jug, lifted the latch and looked in. Gaston was standing in the middle of the room in his shirt-tails, knees apart, feet at right angles, apparently unable to move. On the floor lay the fragmented glory of his new dress uniform. She covered a smile; he looked like a peacock that had met with a serious accident. Of course, he needed to dress up for the Count who was to come to dinner today. But why was he frozen in that extraordinary position?

'Look what I did, Colette, I put on my boots before my breeches, then I tried to get them off, and my spurs caught in the braid of my dolman.' Colette looked behind him. She could see that the spikes of his spurs were entangled in the delicate braid of the glorious silver and blue jacket at his feet. It made her toes curl just to see the damage he would cause if he moved. 'If I pull the braid, I'll be disgraced!' Colette knelt down and disentangled his spurs, carefully easing back the trapped braid as she did so.

'That's it, you're free now; you can take your boots off,' she said.

'That's how I got into trouble in the first place, Colette.' He stood on one leg, grasped the heel of his boot, tried to heave, lost his balance and began to hop backwards.

'Well, don't do it again!' she laughed, snatching away the precious dolman. 'Come, let me take the spurs off first, then I'll pull.' She undid the buckles and removed the wickedly spiked wheels. 'I'm glad I'm not a horse,' she said. Gaston sat down on a chair and held out a boot. She took it in her hands; it was smooth to touch and smelled excitingly of new leather. Then she began to pull.

'It's coming!' Gaston held hard to the sides of his chair, bracing one foot on the floor. The boot came off with an audible 'fop' as the vacuum was released. 'Now for the other one.'

'How will you ever manage on your own?' she asked.

'I may have a servant, otherwise I'll just have to rely on my friends to help.' The second boot proved more difficult. Colette leaned back while Gaston braced himself. 'Pull ... it's coming!' At that moment his stockinged foot slipped away from him on the polished floor, his body weight shifted, the chair tipped forward and the back hit him on the head with a stunning crack. Colette lost her balance and rocketed back with the boot.

'Oh, your poor head,' she said, struggling to her feet. For a second Gaston didn't stir. She threw the boot she was holding to one side and rushed to help him. He stood up groggily, then swayed alarmingly. She grabbed him about the waist and held on. At that moment the door was thrown open and Madame Morteau stood staring at them from the doorway.

'What on earth is going on here!' she demanded. 'Gaston, you should be ashamed ... and in your shirt-tails.' Her look moved to Colette, who didn't dare release Gaston in case he fell. 'Colette, out at once! Have you no sense of propriety!'

'But, Mother, she was only helping me off with my boots!'

'I don't see why that should involve her embracing you about the middle.'

'I fell ... Mother; she's only a ...'

'I don't want to hear about it! The sooner you leave for your regiment the better.' She turned to Colette, who had stepped back, half dismayed, but yet half delighted with the excitement. 'Colette, you are wanted in the kitchen. The Count du Bois will be here shortly. I don't know how you expect poor Margot to prepare dinner on her own. There are still peas to be shelled.'

'Madame, I haven't met the Count. Is he married? Has he children?' Madame Morteau pursed her lips in the way Colette had seen her do when she disapproved of something.

'No, the Count is not married ...' she replied shortly. 'Now, run along.'

Colette hurried off to the kitchen, aware that Madame had answered only part of her question.

CHAPTER 2

Colette Valenod

If Colette had looked out of the landing window as she hurried down to shell peas for the Count, she would have seen a crowd around the statue of St Vincent in the square. Mass was over, and both the villagers and visitors to the Summer Festival were milling about, wondering how to fill the time before the musicians would mount the stand below the statue and the dancing and revelries begin. A man detached himself from the crowd and climbed on to the platform. On his head was a bright red floppy cap, the *bonnet rouge* of the Revolution. He had a waist-length jacket of coarse blue material that opened in front to show a striped cotton waistcoat. Below this were trousers, rather than the stockings and breeches – or culottes – favoured by the aristocracy. This outfit had become the symbol of the Revolution, the dress of the common man in revolt against the aristocracy, and the wearers were known as *sans-culottes*.

Down by the river, unaware of the growing excitement in the square, Jean Brouchard, the miller, stood on the bridge over the millrace, resting his large and comfortable frame against the rail, watching the water hurrying beneath him. Because it was Sunday, the mill was silent. Inside, the huge millstones rested on beds of corn that had been carefully run in just before the stones were stopped the night before. Tomorrow they would start again, with hardly a rumble, rolling easily on the hard grains. But the water in the millrace still flowed, and the huge waterwheel dipped and turned silently on its greased axle, bright curtains of water dropping from its paddles. Today Jean's beard was black. On weekdays it was frosted grey with flour, and his upward curving eyebrows would support little drifts of white. He was slightly deaf from the continuous sounds of the mill, so he didn't hear Lucien, his labourer from the mill, approach at a run.

'Monsieur Brouchard ... Monsieur Brouchard!' The miller turned in surprise; Lucien rarely came near the mill on a Sunday. As an employee, Lucien was a mixed blessing. He was as strong as a horse, but he also had the inclinations of a colt, and was the heart-throb of all the village maidens. As a result, his mind was seldom where it should be – listening to the minute variations of sound that told how the stones were grinding. Jean raised his eyebrows. Lucien went on: 'There is a Jacobin, an *agent provocateur*, addressing the people outside the church. You must come quickly!'

Despite his relaxed appearance, Jean Brouchard was alert. A year and a half ago he had, with some reluctance, agreed to serve as the leader of the village Revolutionary Committee. It was his firm conviction that the Revolution was there to serve the people, rather than the people serving the Revolution, so he had called some meetings to resolve disputes and had spoken loudly and well for liberty, equality and fraternity, and had left it at that. He was, however, well informed. Carters and traders passed through the mill every day. He would sit them on the high stool in his tiny office, where the floor shook and the dust motes danced in the light from cobwebbed windows, and pretend to write in his ledger. As no one could overhear them here, his visitors talked freely. In this way Jean kept abreast of the news that circulated through the network of carters that stretched to the four corners of France.

'Why do you call him an *agent provocateur*?' he asked.

'Because provoking is what he is doing. He's working the people up and trying to get them to start a riot. He knows that the Count is to visit the winery today. He's saying it's a disgrace that the vineyard should be in the hands of one man, an aristocrat and a traitor. He says it should belong to us – the citizens – and that we must confront the Count and demand that the slopes be divided among us.'

'And is anyone listening to him?'

'The village people are laughing behind their hands. They know that there's more to making wine than squeezing grapes into their mouths. But the visitors who have come in for the Summer Festival, and the migrant workers, they are listening.'

'But what can they get out of this? They can't expect to be given slices of land?' the miller protested.

'No, but they can expect a bellyful of wine! That's his line. He's saying that if they march on the winery he will guarantee that they do not go home thirsty.'

'Is he indeed?' Jean straightened himself.

'I *told* you Monsieur Brouchard,' Lucien was getting desperate, 'You must come – now!'

'And you have no interest in a bellyful of wine?'

'Why should I? You know as well as I do that Monsieur Morteau looks after us in the village; it's the rabble that are thirsting.' Lucien, who could actually hear the shouting from the village square, was shifting from foot to foot, but his employer just stood, pushing his hand up under his beard, as he did when thinking. At last he stood away from the rail.

'Listen to me, Lucien. You can't stop a mob, any more than you can stop a mill wheel from turning in a flood; it would be smashed to bits in minutes. What we need is to offer them grist for their mill.'

'I don't understand.'

'I mean something of more substance than wine. Come ... I want you to take a message to the winery. It's for the Count, but give it to Monsieur Morteau, because the Count won't understand. It'll be a chance for you to see young Margot. You have her eating out of your hand, so that can be your reason for going if anyone stops you.'

'She's more likely to bite my hands than to eat out of them!' Lucien looked ruefully at the palms that had so neatly betrayed him on Bernadette's plump back. 'Margot's out for my blood.'

'Well, here's a chance to redeem yourself. Come into the office, I need to write an official letter.' Lucien waited while Jean unscrewed his inkwell, found a piece of paper, flexed his fingers and began to write. He and the vigneron had a long-established understanding of each other, but he must be careful with his words in case the letter fell into the wrong hands. He signed the note, folded it in half, and handed to Lucien. 'Quick now, go! You can tell Monsieur Morteau that this is from me; he will understand.' Jean watched Lucien depart, following one of his night-time routes along the backs of the houses. Then the miller set off for the square with determined strides.

The vigneron's house stood at the top of the village, the main door, which was seldom used, opened on to the sweep of road leading down to the village square. The entrance had been designed for effect, three curving stone steps mounting to a broad platform in front of the door. To the right of the house was a stone archway that led into a cobbled yard. The winery occupied three sides of the yard, while on the fourth was the house. Creepers covered its walls, surrounding the windows and shading the side door, which led, by a short passage, to the kitchen, the nerve centre of the house.

Colette had taken her basket of peas out into the court-yard, away from the heat and activity in the kitchen. It was a spot where they all liked to sit. A trailing vine of jasmine grew against the wall of the house, providing dappled shade. Occasionally it shed little white flowers into her bowl of shelled peas or rewarded her with an intoxicating waft of scent. On the opposite side of the yard were the doorways of the winery, mysterious black caverns. As a child she had not been allowed to join in the festivities of her local grape harvest in case she should witness coarse behaviour, but she felt the air of expectancy that hung over the courtyard, as if it too was looking forward to the activity of the harvest. Nothing much moved today, a couple of chaffinches hopped about, searching for spilled grain between the cob-bles. A sound drifted in from the direction of the village square; it rose and fell rhythmically, reminding her vaguely of the sea.

As she worked, she thought about Gaston and how nice it had been to share something with him. His body had felt strong and firm in her arms when she had steadied him, and she got a closeness and a sense of belonging that she hadn't

felt since she had come to the Morteau household. If only
Gaston could stay. A movement caught her eye. There was a
young man standing in the shadow of the archway, looking
furtively around the yard. She kept still and he didn't appear
to see her. He had good features and an impressive build;
Colette noticed how his shirt bulged where his muscles
pushed at the coarse linen. He didn't look like a thief, but
when he started tiptoeing across the yard towards the open
door of the house, she wondered if she should raise the
alarm. He stopped and ran his fingers through his hair to
smooth it. Then, not satisfied with the result, he spat liber-
ally on his palms and slicked the stray locks into place.
Colette winced, half amused, half disgusted, but she had no
doubt now who their visitor was.

'Monsieur?' she queried. Lucien's jump was so violent that
she started too, accidentally spilling some of her precious
peas.

'*Oh, pardon, Mademoiselle... Je cherche Mademoiselle
Margot?*'

'*Margot est dans la cuisine,*' she said, indicating the door
leading to the kitchen. He bowed nervously, thanked her,
braced himself, and then proceeded with caution into the
house. Colette wanted to see what would happen, but there
were the peas to be picked up. She was still on her hands
and knees when she heard the clatter of approaching
hooves. Before she could rise, the noise reached a cres-
cendo and a carriage hurtled through the arch into the yard,
the coachman hauling back on the reins, and the horses'
shoes knocking sparks from the cobblestones. Almost
before it had stopped, the carriage door flew open and a
man emerged from its dark interior; he must have had the
blinds drawn. He was wearing a wig and was dressed in an

embroidered frock coat. Colette started up; here was someone who was prepared to take the risk of dressing in the
clothes of an aristocrat.

'Bar the gates!' he shouted, as he threw the coat and the
wig into the carriage. 'I'll hold the horses.' The coachman
hurried to close the gates; they were seldom used and pro-
tested loudly. Colette stared at the gentleman. He was a man
of about forty but of athletic build, and he held the horses
competently. He saw her as she stood up, clutching her rescued peas. For a moment their eyes met. His sparked with
interest, but his immediate concerns came first. 'You ...
maid. I need trousers – any trousers – working trousers, not
these damned culottes.' He waved down at his breeches.
Colette, familiar with the voices and ways of the aristocracy,
recognised the new arrival as the Count du Bois, but why
this call for trousers? Colette rather liked being mistaken for
a maid, so she bobbed him a curtsy in her best chamber-
maid imitation before turning towards the door. As she
walked down the short passage that led into the kitchen, a
burst of Margot's richest invective exploded ahead of her,
and her peas were nearly sent flying for a second time as
Lucien, desperately protecting his stomach, backed into her.
Margot, in a fit of righteous fury, was charging at him with
her broom handle. Colette could only retreat ahead of them.

'Oooof, my stomach! *Margot, ma chérie...* I have a
letter... it's urgent.'

'So it wasn't *me* you came to see – you hypocrite! ' They
were all in the open now, where Margot could raise the
broom above her head. As Lucien turned to run he saw
Colette standing nearby.

'Mam'selle,' he shouted at her. '*Excusez-moi...* take this,
it's urgent, it's for Monsieur Mort–' His instructions were cut

short as Margot's broom handle came down with a crack across his shoulders and the note went flying.

'What the hell's going on over there? And where in the name of God are those trousers!' Margot and Lucien, recognising the voice of authority, swivelled as one, frozen in mid-battle, and stared at the irate aristocrat. It was time for Colette to leave; she picked up Lucien's note, dropped it into her bowl, and ran for the kitchen, where she almost bumped into Madame Morteau.

'Where are *you* going, Colette – and where is la Margot?' For one wonderful moment, Colette felt like throwing the bowl – peas, letter and all – over her benefactor, but Madame had her own authority. Colette controlled herself. She needed to think fast; she mustn't get Margot into trouble. Then she remembered the Count and his demand for clothes.

'Madame … it is the Count … he has no trousers!' she exclaimed. If Colette had wanted to stop Madame Morteau in her tracks, she could not have arranged it better. For the first time ever she saw her benefactor at a complete loss for words. She even groped for a chair and sat down.

'The Count … has arrived?'

'*Oui*, Madame.'

'And he has no trousers?'

'*Oui*, Madame… *non*, Madame. He has asked me to get some for him.'

'What then is he wearing?

'Culottes, Madame.' To Colette's amazement a flicker of amusement crossed the stern face.

'Well, thank God for that. To have found you in the company of two trouserless men in one day would have been too much.' She was smiling now. She held up a hand. 'Come, my dear, give me a kiss.' Amazed and pleased,

Colette kissed the upturned cheek. 'Gaston has explained what happened earlier, but now we have work to do. First we must find out why the Count needs trousers.' At that moment there was a clatter of wooden-soled sabots in the passage and Margot burst into the kitchen; the brief moment of harmony was gone.

'*Au secours*! Help, Madame! Madame, there is a mob! They are coming for us. We can't escape.' Margot looked around the room frantically, as if searching for somewhere to hide.

'Calm down, Margot. Now, tell me, *who* is coming for us? What do they want?'

'It's the mob, Madame; they are demanding blood.' Margot rolled her eyeballs so that only the whites showed. Colette felt sick. Her legs gave way and she fell into a chair where she sat, curled up and shaking, as waves of terror swept over her. She could hear the noises from outside now, angry voices raised in disharmony. How could she have mistaken it for the sound of the sea? She dared not close her eyes in case she let in the contorted faces of her dreams. But she sensed when the Count came in – his kind disturbed the air. Madame took control, sending Margot off to get trousers. Where was Monsieur Morteau, she fumed? Why was he never there when there was a crisis? Hazily, Colette recalled the letter that Lucien had been so anxious to deliver. What had she done with it? Fighting back another wave of terror, she remembered, and reached for it from on top of the peas.

'Madame,' she whispered, holding up the note. 'This was brought up by Lucien from the mill. I believe it's for Monsieur–' A hand reached over her shoulder and snatched the note. From the strong scent of pomade she guessed it was the Count.

'Show me that!' He scanned the note quickly. '*Sacré Dieu!* Damn it! It's that damned miller, Brouchard; he is threatening me. He calls me a viper! Confound the man. If I had brought a sword ...'

'*Non ... non ... non ...* swords make for bad pruning,' said Monsieur Morteau, who had come in quietly and was stepping out of his shoes at the door. He offered the Count his hand.

'*Alors, bonjour Monsieur le Comte,*' he said, greeting the Count as he fished in his pocket for his glasses. 'Now, let me see this threatening letter.'

While his vigneron read, the Count paced and turned, jabbing at the note each time he passed. 'He says I'm a snake in the grass and demands me to declare my patriotism. I'll have his mill off him for this!'

Monsieur Morteau held up a hand for silence and began to read aloud:

For the attention of the Count du Bois.

Citoyen ... As chairman of the Revolutionary Committee it is my duty to identify and expose such vipers as pose a threat to our community, and then either destroy them or draw out their poison. At the moment of your arrival it appears that just such a viper has appeared in our midst.

'You see, he means me!' snapped the Count. 'The damned cheek – a viper!'

Monsieur Morteau raised his hand again. 'We should not be too hasty. Perhaps he was afraid that this note might be intercepted. I think it is a warning, not a threat. As Brouchard would say, "look at the flour between the grains."'

'Well, it sounds like a threat to me,' the Count blustered.

Monsieur Morteau read on:

34

Today the citizens gathered for the Summer Festival will march on the winery. You will hear many voices and many demands. I order you not to try, under any circumstances, to buy safety for yourself by offering bribes of land. Neither should you yield to the temptation to curry favour by bribing the people with wine from your cellars.

'What rubbish! I'd shoot the lot of them before I did that; where are my pistols?'

'My dear Count, that is precisely what Brouchard is warning you against. Listen to what he says:

You must realise that it is not your wine but your blood that stands at issue. If you value your lives you will await my command and then declare your patriotism, speaking out for the Revolution and for France.

Yours etc, Jean Brouchard.

'He means that the viper is out there?' The Count asked. There was a surge of shouting outside.

'Precisely, Monsieur le Comte. Listen to them, I think we should go and do what he says. We are all in danger.'

'I still don't like being ordered around by my miller,' protested the Count.

At that moment Gaston spoke from near the door. 'My father is right, we had better go,' he said. 'They will force their way in if we don't.'

They stood immobilised, not by Gaston's words, but by his appearance. To Colette it was as if a peacock had suddenly spread its tail. Even in the relative dark of the room, he glowed, a glorious splash of colour. His trousers were cherry-red, his dolman blue and silver, colours that were repeated in his pelisse, and the shako, which he carried under his arm. His sabre hung low against his sabretache, trailing the ground. Colette blinked.

'Come on, everybody out onto the steps,' the Count ordered, taking command again, hitching his borrowed trousers and busily hiding the lace of his cuffs by rolling up his sleeves. 'I'll give them patriotism!' His hair was short and spiked from the effects of wearing a wig but there was no hiding his authority. As he strode towards the door he grabbed a bottle of wine and a glass from the table, and thrust them into Gaston's hands. Colette followed them in a daze, her feet obeying where her mind failed. There was a howl of derision as the Count led the way out of the door onto the three broad steps before the house. Colette would have turned back if Gaston had not put an arm reassuringly across her shoulders. As the family mustered behind the Count, Gaston moved forward to stand beside him.

'Hurrah for the toy soldier!' someone shouted. Colette, unable to look at the mob, fixed her attention on Gaston's back. Her mind oddly detached, she counted the bands of braid on his back while the leader of the crowd raved. His words meant nothing to her but there was something in their tone that intrigued her. Then she understood; this was how she would have sounded if she had succeeded in using Margot's vulgar language this morning. The man was trying to sound common, but he was no commoner. The crowd was getting bored with his ranting; a coarse voice started calling for wine, and others took up the call. Suddenly a louder voice cut through the clamour.

'Declare yourself, Citizen. Are you a traitor or are you not?'

'It's Brouchard, my miller. Damn him!' Colette heard the Count exclaim. Even the rabble was impressed at the miller addressing his own overlord like this. If the Count had difficulty in swallowing his pride, he didn't show it. On cue, he took a step forward and threw up his arms. He had a deep voice, a strong voice, and he knew how to use it. He also had centuries of authority behind him, just as the listeners, many of them his tenants and labourers, had centuries of subservience. As he spoke, his voice swelled and what he had to say quelled their clamour. He told them about the Prussian invasion that, at that very moment, was taking place on French soil.

'And you,' he said, 'you have the audacity to stand there calling for wine!' He turned to Gaston, who handed him the glass and then filled it to the brim. The Count raised the glass high in front of him. The mob stared up at him, mouths open, as if anticipating some pagan sacrifice.

'This, my comrades, is the blood of Frenchmen. This is the blood of France that at this very minute is being spilled for you and for your country.' He tipped the glass and after the first splash, let a slow thin stream of wine, red as blood, curve from the rim to spatter on the stone steps at his feet. 'And what are you doing for France, what are you doing for the Revolution at this time of danger? I tell you, you are clamouring for wine so that you can wallow in it like pigs until you are insensible.' With that, the Count dashed the last of the wine at their feet. He handed the empty glass to Gaston who stepped to one side and put it and the bottle down.

Exposed by Gaston's sudden move, Colette found herself looking out over the mob, her eyes blurred in denial. The mass swayed like headland corn in a breeze, a motley of fuzzy colours. Here and there were bright splashes of poppy red, the *bonnets rouges,* the caps worn by the Jacobins. Instinct told her that the day still hung in the balance. This was no benign field of corn she was seeing, it was a mob; at a nod it could advance and sweep them all off the steps. She could sense their energy building again, like a dammed stream ready to break its banks. Poor Father, she thought. Is this how he had felt? She wanted to close her eyes, but now Gaston had stepped forward. She stretched out feebly to stop him. He had been so proud of his new cadet's uniform, and now it and he were going to be torn apart.

Brouchard's deep voice rang out again. 'Come on, Toy Soldier. Tell us who you will be fighting for.'

Colette's eyes were riveted on Gaston. The shout was all the encouragement he needed. His head came up, he forced his shoulders back, and the boy became a man. He swept his arms wide, as if he wanted to gather the whole company together as one.

'*Allons, enfants de la Patrie!* Come, children of the Nation.' He shouted. 'I will tell you who I will fight for!' A tingle of excitement ran down Colette's spine. She could feel the fine hairs on the outside of her arms beginning to rise. Then Gaston began to sing, and she heard for the first time the words of the tune he had been trying to remember all morning. His was a young voice, strong and true, and there was a passion behind it that moved them all.

'*Allons, enfants de la Patrie! Le jour de gloire est arrivé ...*'

Gaston, head back, called on the children of the nation, telling them that their day of glory had arrived, and Colette's heart swelled till it nearly burst.

Her fears dissolved and she dared to look down at the mob ... but where *was* the mob? The amorphous, threatening mass had dissolved. These were just ordinary country folk. Among the upturned faces she saw villagers that she knew by sight. Each and every one of them seemed to be reaching up to draw the song down into themselves. There was Nicole from the Boulangerie, and Jean and Luc, two friends who were employed in the winery. That red flag was none other than George Chélon, the blacksmith, delightedly waving his *bonnet rouge* on the end of a pike – the only weapon in sight. Now the tune was changing to the last glorious lines:

'Aux armes, Citoyens! Formez vos bataillons!
Marchons, marchons!...'

Gaston had won their hearts. Grown men mopped their eyes as the boy soldier sang the song through again; they were already mouthing the words, groping to follow the tune. 'Let us march, let's march ...' they wanted it yet again, but Gaston knew when to stop. There was a hesitation, and then a cheer rang out.

'Vive la France... Vive la République... Vive notre petit Hussar!' roared Jean Brouchard, and the whole crowd joined in. Gaston, laughing and blushing, saluted them and, turning to go back into the house, came face to face with Colette. For one long moment their eyes were locked in pure shared happiness, a look that struck deep into both of them. Colette would remember it and treasure it. Gaston would not. In a few hours he would set out into the world to prove himself as a man and as a hussar. He would put away childish things; his romance now was with France. But unknown to him, a tiny shard of that shared moment would remain, lodged deep inside him, where it would act like the grain of sand that provokes an oyster to make a pearl.

Not surprisingly, both the celebratory dinner and Gaston's departure had been delayed. But Gaston was in no hurry, as he planned to spend the night with a friend and had only a few miles to travel. The Count left as soon as dinner was over, saying that he had to see Jean Brouchard. After his departure Colette began to feel more and more of an outsider. This was a time when the family would want to be on their own. So she took a basket, bid Gaston a formal farewell and announced that she was going up to see if the mulberries were ripe. Gaston, who knew the tree, looked up from the saddlebag he was buckling and said that he would wave to her as he passed.

The August sun shed its heat and sank slowly into the western haze, growing huge as it did so. At the edge of the vineyard, under the gnarled and ancient mulberry tree that looked down on the road that Gaston would take, Colette sat waiting.

In the winery the moment of departure came; Gaston kissed his parents an emotional goodbye and swung himself unsteadily into his saddle. Father had opened his 1789 vintage and Gaston was in a pleasant daze. '*Allons, enfants de la Patrie!*' he sang as he rode north.

He never looked up.

The Count called at the mill, ostensibly to thank M. Brouchard for the note he had sent, but really to find out what direction the Jacobin had taken once the riot had broken up. Having established that the man had left, on foot, and was heading south, he laughed and said he was going that way himself and would give him a piece of his mind if he saw him. Working on a hunch, he sat up on the box beside his coachman, looking left and right for anywhere that a coach might have been driven off the road. He guessed that the man was not used to walking in sabots, and was soon proved correct. Tracks showed where a coach and horses had drawn off into the shade of a large oak tree. Leaving his carriage on the road, the Count walked over and found his recent adversary sitting on the coach step, massaging his feet.

'Don't get up,' said the Count pleasantly. 'I know, those sabots are damned uncomfortable.' He bowed. 'Count du Bois at your service, Citoyen. Or is it "Comte" perhaps? Or "Duc"?' He held up a hand. 'No, don't apologise. It is just that I have a feeling that we have certain things in common. Perhaps I can learn from you. Perhaps you also can learn a little from me. Would we be more comfortable, do you think, if we sat in the privacy of your coach?'

At the precise moment when the Count was greeting his adversary, Gaston, now a mile or more from Les Clos du Bois, reined in with an oath; he had forgotten to look up towards the mulberry tree. Colette would have been waiting, and he had never waved. He turned to go back, but realised that she would be gone by now. The sun was sinking behind a distant cloud, sending shafts of light like devil's horns up into the sky. He rode on, dissatisfied with himself, and feeling that he had somehow made a bad beginning to his life as a hussar.

CHAPTER 3

The Road to Amsterdam 1795

'*Vite … vite, dépêchez-vous!* Keep moving. What do you think you are – bloody dragoons? At this rate the army will be in Amsterdam before we catch them!' Lieutenant Gaston Morteau stood high in his stirrups and bellowed down the line. The cavalry horses, bunched together by the sudden halt, shifted restlessly, their hindquarters shuffling sideways, hooves scraping, filling the cold air with the flinty smell of steel on stone. The short plumes on the men's shakos tossed.

Much had happened in the two and a half years since Gaston rode out beneath the mulberry tree without an upward glance. France, having driven the invading army back over the border – without calling on Gaston's help – turned in on itself, and began, with unbelievable ferocity, to devour its own. King Louis was beheaded, as was his wife, Marie Antoinette, and many of the aristocracy. The Jacobin faction, led by the fanatical Robespierre, then attempted to secure the Revolution by fear. Jacobin factions sprang up throughout France, using the guillotine to impose a regime known as *The Terror*. Some of the older regiments, such as the Hussars of Auxerre, stood back, shocked and aloof, while their aristocrat officers slipped quietly away to the safety of exile abroad. In this situation, Gaston, young, able, and patriotic, rose rapidly in rank.

Now with his own command, Gaston found himself on foreign soil and engaged in a real campaign at last. A French army, under the leadership of General Daendels, had crossed the frozen Rhine. Daendels was a leading light in the Dutch Patriot movement, whose slogan was '*People against Princes*,' and whose intention was to topple Stadtholder William V, and thus bring the spirit of the French Revolution to Holland. Gaston had been ordered to join this army and put his small troop of Hussars at the General's disposal; speed was of the essence.

At the head of the column an earnest conversation was taking place between two officer cadets, Marcel Beauchamp and Pierre Colbert, who had taken it upon themselves to halt the column.

'Go on, tell him. I dare you!'

'But, Marcel, what will I say?' the younger boy pleaded.

'Ask him to come quickly. Tell him a lady has fallen into the canal.'

'He'll say it's none of our business.'

'If you think that, Pierre, you don't know our brave lieutenant. Just try it and you'll see. Ask him for orders ...'

'What will you give me?' Pierre demanded, hoping that Marcel's usually precarious finances would put a stop to the dare. Marcel paused for a moment's calculation.

'All right, one louis d'or if you tell him, but you *must* be convincing; he *must* come.'

'Done!' The boys touched hands. Pierre wheeled his horse and set off down the column while Marcel turned to examine the scene of the 'tragedy'. A covered cart lay abandoned on its side in the canal beside the road, where the driver had attempted to escape the advancing troops by driving it over the frozen water. Unfortunately for him, the ice had betrayed him. Some hidden flow or spring had weakened it, the cart had broken through, and now great slabs of ice, like sharks' fins, rose about it in the freezing water. The driver, together with his precious horses, had fled, leaving just one visible casualty, an oil painting in a heavy wooden frame that had floated clear of the cart. The subject of the painting – a girl in a green dress – looked up at Marcel from beneath the water, like drowned Ophelia. A momentary ripple danced over the surface of the canvas and her face took life; it seemed to be appealing to him. Marcel felt uncomfortable and began to have misgivings about his dare. He decided to withdraw to the comparative safety of the head of the column.

Gaston could see the boy – Pierre – galloping down the line towards him, his face flushed with excitement.

'What is it, Colbert?' The boy reined in, tried to salute, but tipped forward and had to grab the pommel of his saddle. Gaston glared at him, 'Lean back while you salute, you sack of potatoes!' The boy righted himself.

'Oh, Lieutenant Morteau, come quickly, sir! There is a woman, sir – a lady. She has fallen into the canal.' Gaston noticed how the soldiers, suddenly interested, turned in their saddles. He kept his eyes on the boy.

'Well, have you got her out?' he snapped.

'No, sir. The water is too deep!'

'Can't you swim?'

'Yes, sir. But it's too ...' The boy blundered to a halt. 'We ... we need your orders, sir.'

All Gaston's instincts told him that the boy was up to something. The lad was, after all, no more than a reflection of what he himself had been like when he joined the Hussars – a carefree happy-go-lucky youngster on the brink of

an adventure. But that was before the *noyades* – the drownings – when the innocent cadet that had been Gaston
Morteau had been obliterated forever. He slammed the door
on that memory, and pulled the head of his little mare out
from the line. His first duty was to young Pierre; one way or
the other Pierre would have to learn that a good officer must
take seriously what his subordinate tells him, no matter how
outlandish it might seem. He glared at the lad, and touched
his horse's sides with his spurs. His mare, which had hardly
felt a spur since he bought her, leapt forward, forcing Pierre
to rear his horse out of their way. Gaston thundered down
the line. As he approached the head of the column, he could
see the capsized cart, looking like a foundered ship. He
reined back, sending stones skittering over the shattered ice.
Perhaps there really had been an accident.

'Where is she, then?' he shouted, looking for ripples, for
any sign of someone struggling. He turned to the silent
ranks. The pale face of Cadet Beauchamp stood out like a
beacon from among the grinning soldiers. Silently the boy
pointed to the water. The lieutenant followed the line of his
finger to where, just beneath the surface, a picture floated,
face up. He had been right, it was a prank, but even so, the
sight of that picture affected him strangely. He could see the
girl, just as Marcel had seen her a moment before, startled
into apparent life by the moving water that seemed to ruffle
the green silk of her dress. There was a suppressed snort of
laughter from the ranks.

Suddenly Gaston felt the hot blood of anger suffusing his
face. For the past year he had clung to chivalry as his only
protection against the horrors of civil war. For him a soldier
had two alternatives: to become a monster, or to preserve
his sanity within a shell of impeccable behaviour. He

schooled himself; he must not turn. The obvious thing to do was to ride on, to ignore the men, and to discipline the boys later. But the laughter would still be there. Damn the boys! They should be flogged, but how were they to know that his elaborate façade – his moustaches, his swagger – had a purpose, not just for him, but for them also. He would not have them turned into monsters!

'Here,' he snapped at Marcel. 'Hold my mare.'

Pierre rode up. 'You, Colbert, my pelisse, my shako.' He wouldn't stoop to removing his trousers. In dismayed horror, the boys took his fur-lined cloak and cap and held his horse. It was Pierre who cracked first.

'Sir … I'll go, sir.'

'You had your chance, Colbert, and you did not take it.' Gaston lowered himself into the water; it was so cold it almost burned. It was also deeper than he had expected; it was not a drainage ditch, but a canal that had been dredged to take barges. He took a deep breath and struck out for the picture, forcing down the rafts of ice. He covered the distance in only a stroke or two, but the cold hit him like a hammer blow. He seized the picture, turned in a fury of water, and was back in seconds. Eager hands stretched out to relieve him of his burden, and then to haul him out. He stood on the bank, willing himself not to shiver, and pulled his clothes over his streaming body. He took his cloak and shako, and looked coldly at the two boys. A cheer went up from the old hands in his troop behind. He didn't even blink. The soldiers, bless them, took him at face value, regarding his chivalry as a source of entertainment.

'Take the lady,' he said to the boys. 'Secure her to a remount so the men can see her. Stay at her side, and if anyone shows her the slightest disrespect you are to defend her honour with your lives.' He swung himself into the saddle. '*Avancez*!' The familiar rattle of cavalry in advance was reassuring. In the distance a windmill turned lazily in the scarcely breathing air and Gaston thought wryly of a lean and foolish Spanish knight.

'Gaston, my young friend! Lord save us, you were a lad of sixteen when I saw you last!'

'General! Come in please. Sit down, sit down. I have ordered hot punch – I am frozen – will you join me?' General Daendels had stayed with the Morteau family back in 1789, while in exile from Holland for his political views. When the Revolution broke out in Paris he thought it best to leave the capital and, finding himself near the vineyards of Les Clos du Bois, had introduced himself to M. Morteau, who was known to him as a winemaking legend. As he said himself, he came for the day and stayed for two months.

'I'll join you with pleasure.' The General doffed his hat and stood stroking its blue white and red cockade while he looked around. 'So, what have you been up to, Lieutenant? I have had at least two complaints that your young coxcombs have been challenging my men over some lady of yours?'

'Have they indeed?' said Gaston with a laugh. 'Excuse me, General, while I call them off. Raoul!' he shouted. His servant appeared. 'Go and tell Beauchamp and Colbert that they are to bring her ladyship up here, at the double.' Raoul looked puzzled. 'Go on, they will know what I mean, and be careful what you say, or they will run you through.' He turned to the General. 'We had a little rescue today. I have hardly had a chance to look at her. But tell me, do we march on Amsterdam?'

'No, not yet. We wait here in Maarssen. I am sending Adjutant Krayenhoff into the city under flag of truce. If he can persuade the City Council to resign, the Stadtholder will be out, and we will then do business with the Pro-Patriots; there will be no need for war.'

'Oh good ... excellent,' Gaston said enthusiastically.

The General raised an eyebrow. 'I have heard that you do a fine line in chivalry, Gaston, and promoted lieutenant already! Not spoiling for a fight, then?'

'No, General. After witnessing Frenchmen fighting Frenchmen, I have no illusions about war. If we can bring you victory without unsheathing our swords, all the better. As for the promotion, I have been lucky. Many of my senior officers were Royalists at heart. When the King was exe-cuted they fled for England, so there was no choice but to promote me. No, give me victory without war any day.'

'Amen to that.' There was a clatter on the stairs.

'Careful as you bring her up,' shouted Gaston.

'What? Is the poor lady in a litter, then?'

'A litter? Oh, I never explained,' Gaston laughed. 'My latest conquest, she's a picture.' A small procession entered the room. Marcel came first, hand on sabre, then Raoul – small and bandy legged – carrying the portrait, and lastly Pierre, backing in at the door as if completing a rearguard action. 'Prop her up here, Raoul, at the foot of my bed.' The Lieutenant turned to introduce the two boys: 'Cadet Beauchamp, Cadet Colbert ... meet General Daendels.' The boys sprang to attention and saluted. The General acknowl-edged their salute with a nod, but he seemed more inter-ested in the painting.

'Good heavens, Morteau, where did you find this gem? Look at her! She is Dutch – of course she is – her hair, her skin. Haven't I stared calf-eyed across the aisle in church at girls such as this? Look at her dress, yards of priceless green silk – a painter's nightmare. But it's the girl that holds my eye. See how she leans forward, as if she has just made some point in argument, to her lover perhaps. Poor fool, he'd have to have his wits about him. I wonder what was the occasion for the portrait? The artist often leaves clues about his subject, you know.' The General was leaning close, examining the canvas, inch by inch. 'This is unusual ... for a girl, that is. You see, there are books – so we know she can read – but not books on etiquette or house management, as you might expect for a young bride. And look, here is a globe and, if I'm not mistaken, a telescope. A young astronomer perhaps, but also a musician – the guitar and the pretty spinet tell us that. Now, what about the painting hanging on the wall? It's a seascape so that could mean a lover across the seas, but the sails are aslant so it may not be plain sailing. Wouldn't it be nice to know who she was?'

'Her name is Louise, sir!' A strangled voice interjected. Gaston had forgotten about the boys, and the interruption reminded him of their misdemeanour. He turned. Both cadets stood stiff as ramrods.

'Who said you could put a name to her, let alone speak?' He noticed Pierre blushing to the roots of his hair. 'Well?'

'Sir, it's ... it's inscribed on the urn, sir, on its plinth. It says "Louise", sir.'

'It does, you know,' agreed the General, examining the urn, which stood as a centrepiece to the arrangement on the table. Then he straightened his back. 'But you still haven't told me how you came by this lady.'

Before Gaston could reply, Pierre blurted out, 'Lieutenant Morteau jumped into the canal and saved her, sir.' The admiration in his voice was evident.

'Colbert!' Gaston said sharply. 'Who gave you permission to speak?'

'Well, Lieutenant,' said the General, 'I envy you your prize. But, as you rescued her, then she rightfully belongs to you. Mind that you keep her safe.' He smiled at the portrait. 'No beauty, but definitely a girl of character.'

Out of the corner of his eye, Gaston noticed the boys stiffen. To his horror, young Colbert even made a gesture towards his sword! It was high time they left.

'Enough!' He ordered. 'Cadets, dismiss!' They turned to the door. 'And don't drag your sabres down the steps!' he called after them. He turned to the General with a laugh. 'You shouldn't have said that she was no beauty, sir. You were in danger of your life. It would be a bad start to 1795 if you were sliced up by two of my clowns.' The door darkened and Raoul appeared with a steaming jug and two glasses. 'Ah … the punch at last. By God, but I need this; that canal water has me chilled to the bone.'

'*Proost!* As we say here in the Netherlands. Here's to your promotion,' the General raised his glass, 'and I don't accept that nonsense about them *having* to promote you; I have heard good reports of you.' The General drank. 'So, are your parents well? I have not forgotten your family's kindness to me. How have they coped with the Terror? I just don't understand you French: the most civilised nation in the world and you have to start cutting off each other's heads.'

'With a humane beheading machine,' Gaston said uneasily.

'You tell that to the poor wretch on the tumbrel on his way to be guillotined! Hopefully, with the beheading of Robespierre in July, the worst is over. Did it affect you at home?'

'On the day I left, we had an incident that could have turned nasty,' Gaston said. 'An *agent provocateur* came into the village and tried to stir up trouble. Looking back, it was a timely warning. I've been back since then; everything was all right at home. You remember the Count? Well, he has declared for the Revolution, and still lives in the chateau, but now as its 'caretaker'. However, I am not fully up to date; my mail has been chasing after me ever since I left Auxerre a year ago. It missed me in Nantes, and again in Paris, but I was hoping it would be here.'

General Daendels drained his glass. 'I'll ask after your mail, but I'd better go now. You look done in lad, go and get some rest.'

When the General had departed, Gaston suddenly felt exhausted. His trousers were still damp from his ducking and seemed to be sucking the warmth out of his body.

'No more visitors, Raoul. I am going to bed.'

'What'll I say to them as wants you, sir?'

'Tell them what you like,' groaned Gaston, pulling off his shirt and waving Raoul away. The shivers that he had managed to suppress during the General's visit were now coming over him in waves. He stripped down to his trousers and began to open his buttons. He was about to push them down when something made him uneasy; he had a distinct feeling of being watched. He looked at the portrait. The girl returned his gaze. Feeling more than a little foolish, he picked up his shirt, draped it over the picture and finished undressing. Then he discovered he had nothing to put on.

'Raoul!' he shouted down the stairs. 'Where's my nightshirt?'

'Coming, sir.'

Down below, someone was demanding to see him. Gaston grinned as he heard Raoul snap, 'No, you can't. The lieutenant is entertaining a lady.' Raoul stamped up the stairs and threw his nightshirt onto the bed. 'I was a-heating of it in front of the fire,' he said defensively and began to pick up Gaston's scattered garments. 'Look at the mess your trousers is in, sir,' he grumbled. At that moment he saw Gaston's shirt hanging over the picture and plucked it away. Gaston covered himself involuntarily:

'Don't do that, you fool. Can't you see I'm naked?'

Raoul looked at him in astonishment.

'Mad … bleeding mad,' he said aloud as he closed the door, and left Gaston to pull his nightshirt over his head.

Gaston sank back in the bed. This was one of the best billets he had had for a long time; it even had a feather mattress. But he would find no comfort in its softness tonight. The fever that he had been holding back all day was tightening its grip. He felt lightheaded and dizzy. As the room began to swim, he fixed his gaze on the girl in the portrait. Bent forward like that, it was almost as though she was reaching out to him …

'Don't go … stay with me!' he whispered out loud, but his voice was lost in the long plunge down into his own private hell.

Raoul pressed a cloth, damp with vinegar, on Gaston's burning forehead.

'Bless you sir,' he said soothingly, 'they were troubled times indeed.' Marcel and Pierre, overcome with guilt at having been the cause of their lieutenant's sickness, stood and watched dejectedly. It was Gaston's third day of fever.

Suddenly the sick man sat up straight in bed. His eyes glowed like coals in their dark sockets.

'Listen boys, listen. Those aren't sea creatures, those are human voices, and they're from the *noyades*. Listen ... can't you hear?' He held up a hand, commanding silence. 'Now ... "*Vive le Roi*".' He turned towards them, cupping his hand around his ear as if straining to hear. Then he shook his head sadly and whispered, '*Rien* ... nothing ... no more'. Raoul clicked his tongue as if he knew what Gaston was talking about. Then Gaston turned his head and vomited out in one long cruel retch into Raoul's basin.

'You'll feel better after that,' Raoul said approvingly.

The Lieutenant sank back on the pillows, and the boys stood by helplessly, as if their spurs were nailed to the floor. After a while Raoul placed his hand on Gaston's forehead. He checked his palm. Then he hurriedly dried his hand on his trousers, and laid it back on his officer's forehead. A broad grin cut his ugly little face.

'He's sweating lads, he's bloody sweating! His fever's broke.' The battle-hardened little soldier-turned-servant banged his knee with his fist and then wiped his eyes on his sleeve. They all waited hopefully until at last Gaston's breathing slowed into a deep natural sleep. The boys turned to go, but Marcel had a question for Raoul.

'Raoul,' he whispered. 'What are the *noyades?*'

Raoul whipped around. 'Don't you ask that, boy. Not never, understand? It were in Nantes, before you joined. It cut us all up, him most of all.'

At last Gaston was dreaming normally. The horrors of his delirium were now replaced by delicious feelings of content. He was dreaming of home, a boy again, listening to the chatter and clatter of the grape pickers setting out for the slopes. Perhaps he had been sick, because someone was sitting beside him, Mother probably, sewing. He would keep his eyes tight shut; she wouldn't go away then.

He must have woken, because he heard Raoul's voice complaining that it was snowing. This time his mind floated off to an earlier dawn and a younger boy, waking to find his room filled with a magical translucent light. The young Gaston lay there, staring at the ceiling, wondering where the strange light was coming from. Then he hopped out of bed, threw the casement wide, and saw, for the first time in his life, a whole world turned white with snow. He looked up towards the vineyards that lined the shallow cup in which his village lay; to his amazement the vines had gone. But they couldn't have disappeared! He searched the slopes until at last, where the sun was glancing low over the snow, he saw, like secret writing, soft lines of shadow, the regimented lines of vines beneath.

The scene changed, and the snow became one vast sheet of paper. Cadet Gaston Morteau was about to sit his written examination for the rank of sub-lieutenant. He appeared to be the only candidate. At a high desk in front of him sat his examiner, an ancient general, his sagging jowls giving him the look of a bloodhound.

'Cadet Morteau,' said the general with a sigh, as if Gaston was already a lost cause. 'You are a dreamer and therefore quite unsuited to be an officer of Hussars.' He laboriously placed his fingers together so that they formed a tent in front of his face. 'At this point in time, Cadet Morteau, you are in a dream. In other words, you do not actually exist.' Gaston was relieved to know it was just a dream, at least he could wake up. 'For your examination today,' the General continued, 'your task will be to create the person you really are. Do I make myself clear?'

'You mean, sir, the person who is dreaming my dream?'

'Precisely. It is the reverse of your un-soldierly habit of constantly dreaming that you are someone who you are not.'

'But sir ... what if I should wake up before I am finished?'

The General's eyes glinted red and something that might have been a smile contorted his face.

'Cadet Morteau ... how *can* you wake up before you have created yourself? You have just one hour – starting *now!*' He reached out for a huge hourglass that stood on the desk beside him and turned it with a thump. Gaston jumped; the sand was already cascading through the glass. Sweat sprang out on his forehead. Who am I? He looked around desperately for something to write with. It was all there: quill, penknife, ink, sand. He hacked at the quill, hoping that inspiration would come while he fashioned a nib, but his mind was as blank as the vast sheet of paper before him. He dipped his nib, but still couldn't think of anything to say. He stared at the paper. Perhaps his story was there, hidden, like the vines beneath the snow. He tilted the sheet towards the light; but still there was nothing. The General coughed and tapped the hourglass.

Somewhere in the present-day building, someone, Raoul perhaps, dropped a saucepan.

Gaston opened his eyes and lay staring up at the ceiling. His first feeling was one of relief at having woken at all; he had thought that he was trapped in that dream forever. Out of the corner of his eye, he sensed that there was someone sitting beside him. He turned, expecting to see Raoul, but it was a woman ... a girl really. She smiled at him. Her face seemed familiar, but he could not place her just at the moment. He felt his eyes closing, but then he remembered his dream, and opened them again quickly; he didn't want to go back to that.

'Forgive me,' he said, 'but do I know you?'

'I'm Louise Eeden, the girl you rescued from the canal.'

'Oh God ...' he groaned.

'I'm sorry... would you like me to go?'

'Oh no, please stay. It's just that ... I thought I had woken, but I must still be dreaming. The General did tell me that I couldn't wake up until I had written my story.'

'That sounds interesting,' the girl said, leaning forward. 'Tell me about your dream.'

Gaston explained, as best he could, about the General and the examination he had to undergo. Rather to his surprise, she laughed. 'My father told me about a philosopher once who said that perhaps we are all part of someone else's dream. But I don't think you can be expected to write your own story. We do that by living. Maybe someone else is trying to write your story and is waiting for you to decide who you really are. In any event, I think you can consider yourself awake now.'

Gaston thought about this; then he smiled ruefully. 'But if I'm awake you'll have to go, won't you – and I may never see you again?'

'You'll have my picture. Anyway, you may not want me around; I may just be part of your fevered imagination. Close your eyes ... I'll stay here, but only if you want me.' Gaston closed his eyes. It was all too much for him, but somehow he felt happier than he had in ages and soon slipped into a deep and restorative sleep.

As Louise watched the young man sleeping, she wondered about her presence here. She thought back to the only time, since the explosion in Delft, when she had really 'lived' in someone else's mind. After the catastrophe, Master Haitink, the artist who had painted her portrait, had gone into a decline. But while his body failed, his mind remained strong; Louise's image grew to be so vivid in his memory that he began to see her as if in life. During that year – as the town of Delft froze in grief – Louise came and sat with the old man, just as she was sitting now with this young French officer, trying to be a comfort and a real presence for him. When eventually the Master passed away, she was by his side.

It was Pieter, the Master's apprentice, who had finished Louise's portrait after Master Haitink's death, but because he had no indentures and no master, he could neither teach nor sell his own paintings. It had been a dreadful time. Time and again, racked with grief, Pieter had tried, in his own way, to do what the Master had done: recreate Louise in his mind as he worked, but their love had been too real to allow regeneration, their time together too precious. The pain of another parting would destroy Pieter. So she held back, and as time passed, she saw the possibility of a new love emerging for him. After the Master's death Pieter had stayed on as a watchman and helper in the public house. Tongues began to wag at his continued presence in the house of the young widow. Mistress Kathenka was not yet forty when she and Pieter married. Though initially a marriage of convenience, it soon matured to love, and Louise was glad for Pieter. It was only when he picked up his brushes to work on her portrait for the last time, however, and painted her name on the plinth of the urn, that the pain of her death finally left him, and the magic and wonder of their lives together burst in on him. There was nothing more Louise could do for him now, so she, who had never longed for heaven, settled for oblivion.

And that was how it was. Once Pieter was gone, her picture, without the Master's signature, was not valued. She was passed from hand to hand, an object to hang on the wall; people liked the green of her dress. No one else had the eyes to see beyond the surface of the painting and engage with the girl the Master had painted. The silence that she had chosen seemed to be without end or echo, except for one small occasional noise, which intrigued her. It was a sound not unlike the whisper of a pen on paper.

Now Louise turned to look at the face of the young man who had rescued her from the canal. He wasn't much older than Pieter. As he slept she could see health and vigour returning to his face. Was her presence here just an accident born out of his fever? Would he want her around once he had recovered or would she once again be consigned to her portrait? She remembered what the Master had predicted about his painting of the Beggar at the Beginhof Gate – a flea-ridden old man with a beautiful singing voice: 'There will be those far down the river of time perhaps, who will bring the old boy back to life for us. Who knows but that someone may even hear him sing.'

Suddenly Louise was filled with hope.

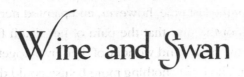

CHAPTER 4

Wine and Swan

The cheering spread ahead of Adjutant Krayenhoff as he rode in triumph into the village of Maarssen. The Stadtholder had fled and Amsterdam was in the hands of the Pro-Patriots. Even while the adjutant was reporting the success of his mission to General Daendels, Cadet Colbert was pounding up the stairs to Gaston's room, quite ignoring Raoul's protests.

'Nonsense, Raoul, of course he will want to know!' He burst into the room with a clash of spur and sabre. 'Sir, Krayenhoff's back, the Pro-Patriots have taken over. *Vive la France!*' He waved his hat, but the ceiling was low and he was rewarded with a shower of loose plaster. 'But wouldn't it make you sick, sir!'

'Sick, Marcel?'

'Pierre and me were planning on some action, sir. We reckoned we could slice up these Dutch burghers like sausages.'

'Don't you believe it. They didn't create an empire by sitting on their backsides. Anyway, General Daendels is Dutch, as apparently is Mademoiselle Louise here. So be careful who you plan to slice.'

'Oh, indeed, sir,' said Marcel, unabashed and happy to put his patriotism to one side. 'Glad you're better, sir.' He turned to the portrait. 'Could we take her, sir, Pierre and me?

We thought we could get the carpenter to make a case for her, with oiled cloth inside, so she doesn't get wet.'

'So you think I should keep her, then?'

'Of course!' said the boy, horrified. 'We ... well, I mean you, rescued her, sir.' He blushed to his ears. 'Pierre and me's really sorry sir, we didn't mean ...' Gaston managed to glare at him.

'I'll consider your behaviour later. In the meantime, yes you may take her; it will give me an opportunity to get dressed.'

'What ... ?' Marcel looked puzzled.

'Oh go on ... go!' Gaston snapped. 'I just need to get my legs under me, that's all.'

'Raoul, no ... no... don't let go. I'm a sick man, remember.' Gaston, somewhat dishevelled, in his dress uniform, stood swaying in the doorway of his bedroom. General Daendels's celebratory dinner was over; tomorrow Gaston's hussars would head south as escort to the officer delegated to bring the good news to Paris.

'Pissed out of your mind, you are sir, and that's the truth,' Raoul responded, unimpressed. His campaign against Gaston's ego was single-minded but private. Woe betide anyone, of any rank from general down, who said a word against his lieutenant.

'Nonsense. Look, I can stand,' said Gaston. 'But I am the one constant point in a world gone mad. Are we in an earthquake?'

'No, sir.' Raoul detached Gaston's hand and put it against the wall.

'Swan. Have you ever tasted swan, Raoul? Krayenhoff's

men found two swans frozen into a canal on their way back from Amsterdam. Served them dressed up in their own skins, feathers and all. Set them sailing down the table in majesty. Tough as old boots, actually. Must have been starving, the poor creatures. So, Amsterdam has fallen and I never even unsheathed my sword!'

'Just as well, if you ask me,' Raoul commented dryly, stepping back to see if Gaston could be left unsupported.

'Ha! You're right, the devils wouldn't have had a chance,' Gaston chuckled as Raoul made himself busy at the bed. 'Remember the engagement at the Pont de Chasse, Raoul, and that black-visaged Royalist I downed?'

'I remember you falling off your horse, sir.'

'Nonsense, I threw myself on the man.' Gaston started some complicated manoeuvres with his sheathed sabre, bracing it against the floor so that it acted as a third leg. 'Look ... steady as a rock now. I learned this from Commandant Pêche – the old soak.' Gaston gazed about the room and then noticed, for the first time, that the boys had returned the portrait of the Dutch girl. It was standing at the end of his bed; they had had a travelling case made for it, which, when opened up, stood on three legs like an easel. Gaston blinked, the girl's face was curiously animated by the moonlight breaking through the uneven glass of the window. He bowed to her, feeling embarrassed and a little ashamed at his condition.

He said to himself: 'Now, how am I to get undressed?' Unfortunately Raoul heard him; he threw down the pillow he had been straightening and turned on him in irritation. Nursing his officer was one thing, but he was damned if he was going to start undressing him.

'On your own, sir!' he flared. 'Anything else?'

'A little punch?' Gaston asked hopefully as Raoul brushed past and clattered dismissively down the stairs.

Gaston turned to the portrait. 'Mademoiselle Louise, your servant. I'm sorry you find me ... shall we say ... incapacitated. I will recover my dignity in due–' He was bending to deliver one of his specially deep bows when he heard a laugh, a girl's laugh, somewhere in the room. He whipped about, trying to place the sound. Perhaps one of the street women had followed him up the stairs. But that was no whore's cackle; it was a clear liquid laugh that made him want to smile.

'Oh, but I like you without your dignity!'

And there she was – the girl from the picture – sitting on the chair beside his bed, just as she had been when he was sick. For an instant Gaston saw, as others had seen before, a flash of beauty as transitory and as intense as a jewel tossed in the air. He gasped, his sword slipped, and he lost his balance. He struggled to recover. She must be a hallucination; perhaps it was the effects of the swan. He wanted to look again ... but yet he dared not. He scrabbled blindly towards the door.

'Raoul!' he bellowed down the stairs, then covered his mouth. What if Raoul came up? A door was snatched open below and Raoul's voice rasped up the stairs.

'Holy mother of God! What is it now?'

'Er ... forget about the punch,' he called weakly, and winced as the door slammed below. He turned and peered cautiously back into his room. She hadn't gone; she was still there, looking about her. Gaston found refuge in his innate good manners. He addressed her from the door: 'Mademoiselle, I believe it was you who came and sat with me when I was sick?' She turned with a smile.

'Yes, you asked me to, if you remember.'

'Did I? … I was so grateful for your company.' He moved back into the room tentatively, as if his rights there were now uncertain. He had a soldier's ability to sober up in a crisis and he was beginning to think clearly now, even if everything appeared a little bit brighter, a little bit sharper than usual. 'May I close the door?' Perhaps she would think it improper to be alone with a man. There was a chair near the window. He crossed to it and sat down. 'Forgive me, Mademoiselle. You see, I thought you were a dream. I had many dreams during my fever.'

'Yes, I know,' the girl said. Gaston looked at her warily.

'You had that strange dream about your examination,' she went on, 'how you had to invent yourself by writing your own story?'

'Ah, *that* dream,' he felt relieved. 'Did I really tell you about that …? It was silly.'

'Oh no, it told me a lot about you. I think we should listen to our dreams … What were the *noyades?*' The room reeled and darkened for Gaston.

'No!' he said, sharply. 'Don't talk of such things!' He saw her wince but couldn't stop. 'It is none of your business!' He thrust his hands between his knees and clamped them there as the black clouds of depression boiled up inside him. After a while he raised his eyes. The girl was staring at the thread-bare carpet, stricken, her eyes brimming. He wanted to reach out and take her hand; she seemed so real. Then something else occurred to him. 'Excuse me, Mademoiselle, you are Dutch, I believe? How are you able to understand me, then, when I am speaking French?' A frown crossed the girl's face and he thought she looked, if anything, more beautiful when she was serious.

'I don't know. I learned some Latin from my father, but not French. And you are right – I am Dutch – Louise Eeden from Delft. But please call me Louise. Maybe I can understand you because it is your mind that is recreating me from my portrait. It feels to me as if you are giving me the means to communicate with you. However, you don't seem to have taken my free will.' A mischievous smile flickered across her face. 'You may live to regret that! But seriously, however you are doing it, I am truly grateful to you, both for the gift of life and the gift of language.'

Sober, Gaston might have questioned her explanation, but another practicality had just occurred to him. Here she was, a vulnerable girl alone in the room of a soldier about whom she knew absolutely nothing.

'But, Mademoiselle Louise, isn't it a terrible risk for you? If *I* can recreate you, couldn't any old scoundrel do the same, and then ... how shall I say... impose himself on you?' To his surprise, she laughed.

'Monsieur Gaston, I assure you, after the silence of a century I would be happy to be recreated in a robber's den. And I have a feeling that Master Haitink, who painted me, may have taken care of that situation ...'

Her voice trailed off. Gaston looked up; she was staring into the distance, as if looking back down the tunnel of time. When she spoke again her voice was softer, a little sad, but full of affection. 'The old man who painted my portrait loved me, Monsieur Gaston, and I him, even though we were like Greek warriors prepared for a fight at the smallest slight. And he painted me as I was – not as I, nor even as he – would have liked me to be. I am beginning to believe that in order for anyone to give me life, they must *want* to do so. And who would want a plain, argumentative little Dutch girl?' The girl smiled to herself, 'Thanks to the Master, I suspect I am quite safe, really.'

'Well, I can tell you that my two boys are stricken with you.'

'Pierre and Marcel? They're sweet. Pierre reminds me of someone I knew – Pieter – not in looks, but in character.' Almost to herself, she added: 'I must be careful.'

'Was Pieter a friend of yours?'

'Oh yes. Pieter was the Master's apprentice. We were...' but Louise wasn't able to finish, and the statement hung between them like an unresolved chord.

'It was not to be ... this friendship?' Gaston asked. Louise shook her head and smiled sadly:

'No, it was not to be,' she sighed.

If Gaston had been completely sober he probably would not have pursued the matter, but then neither would she have answered him so freely. 'Can you tell me what happened?' he asked sympathetically.

'I was killed,' Louise said.

She hadn't meant to shock, but she heard Gaston's sharp intake of breath. 'It was a gunpowder explosion ... an accident, I believe.'

'But that's terrible!' He seemed genuinely upset. 'Did you suffer?'

'No ...' Louise replied. 'In a strange way I think I was too interested in what had happened to feel anything for myself.' She beckoned Gaston closer and he drew his chair nearer the bed, listening in silence as she told him about the immediate aftermath of the explosion. She described how her soul had lingered, floating high over the shattered town of Delft.

'You see, Gaston,' she said, 'It was all so sudden. One

minute I was carrying a hot drink in to my sick mother, and the next I was looking down on the wreckage of the town as a bird might see it. I was amazed and fascinated. My first impulse was to show it to my father. He was a master potter, but he was also a man of science; he would have been so interested and would have pointed out all sorts of things.' She sighed wistfully. 'As I looked down I could see that the pall of smoke and dust over the town was thinning. Something terrible had happened down there, but yet I was detached from it; people were running, but in no particular direction. I recognised the market place where the Master had his studio. The houses there were still standing but slates kept falling from the roof of the nearby Church, the Nieuwe Kerk, in noisy cascades. It was strange, this seemed to be the only sound: the rattle and clatter of falling slates and tiles. Then I recognised another, softer sound,' Louise shook her head in wonder as she remembered. 'It was the sound of sweeping. It was the *huisvrouwen* of Delft: unable to comprehend the enormity of the disaster that surrounded them, they were finding escape in the familiar and in what they did best by sweeping up the glass and the twisted lead from their broken windows.'

'I *had* to know what had happened. There must be some explanation for the incredible devastation below. There is a river that runs around three sides of Delft: the Vliet or Schiekanaal. I could see the sweep of it, looking for all the world like an embracing arm supporting the poor, crippled town. Timbers and horrible things were bobbing on its surface. But where was the gunpowder magazine and the firing range that I used to look into from my bedroom? Where were the magnificent trees that had shaded them? There was an old thrush that used to sing to me in those trees ... gone!

Where, oh where, was my home?' Louise dropped her voice. 'You know, I couldn't even tell where our house had stood. All I could see was a mighty pit where the gunpowder magazine had been. Gradually it came to me what had happened. The magazine had blown up.'

Gaston was leaning forward, hands on the hilt of his sabre, willing her to go on.

'I could hear a distant clock chiming. I counted – was that eleven? Then I waited for the carillon on the Nieuwe Kerk, but no chime came; the bells must have been knocked off their pivots. What was I doing up here? Should I be going somewhere? I looked up at the arched dome of the sky. Was heaven up there? Was that hell below? Then I realised that there were other presences up there with me – other victims of the blast. Some seemed to know where they were going, as if fulfilled by their own concepts of heaven. Others, like me, were drifting. Just then I felt a stronger presence rising towards me; here was a soul with purpose. My heart gave a lurch, there was only one person it could be, my old nurse, Annie. No one but she could keep her identity intact at a moment like this.

'I wish you could have met her, Gaston. You see, Annie was a Calvinist, therefore she *knew* that there would be a place laid for her at the Lord's table.' Louise smiled at the memory. 'She rose towards me, glowing with purpose, determined not to disappoint her Lord by delaying on the way. But yet, when she saw me she hesitated. Even then, she was prepared to be late for the Lord in order to lift me back onto the path of righteousness: "Go on Annie," I called to her. "Dear Annie, God is waiting for you." She gave me one last long look of love and then she was off, like a star diminishing into heaven.'

'Then what happened?' Gaston urged, breaking the ensuing silence.

'I wondered if I should follow Annie? But what would I *do* in heaven? Annie's belief in God and heaven was so different from mine. A terrible loneliness gripped me then, and I was like a small child again, longing for my mother. I looked about me wildly; of course, she must have died too!

"Where are you, Mother?" I called. As if in answer, I found myself remembering one day in spring, when I was little, lying on a canal bank and breathing, for the very first time, the scent of early primroses. Mother was watching me, smiling, and I knew that this was her idea of heaven. Suspended there above the town, I breathed in, and yes, there it was, the scent of primroses. I spread my arms wide and her essence was all around me. This would be Mother's way. To dispense her soul as a scent on the wind, expending her love in one profligate outpouring until her last atom was gone and she was at once everywhere and nowhere. "Goodbye Mother," I whispered to the wind.

'I could guess now where Father would be. He and God would be side by side down there where the soil still reeked, sleeves rolled up, working unseen with victim and helper alike. I remember wondering if Father would be able to stop himself from quizzing his celestial partner for information on some matter of science, or on the creation.

'So they all had their chosen place – except me. There was only one place I wanted to be and that was in the arms of Pieter, the Master's apprentice, alive and able to be loved again. But then I knew that this, of all heavens, was the one to be denied me.'

'It was then – only then – that I realised that I had died and that I could never be with Pieter again. After all we had been through, when it seemed certain that we could finally be together, it had all been taken away. How I longed to hold him in my arms and to join with him, as I never had in life, but I hadn't much time left; I could feel my energy draining away. There was nothing to sustain me there above the ruin of my town; it was as if the pen that had been writing my story had paused, waiting for me to decide. Then, at last, I remembered my portrait and what the Master had said when he had finally achieved my likeness: "One day, three hundred years from now, more perhaps, people will see this canvas and you and I – Louise – we will live again." So there was a place where I had an entity – a place where I had a right to be – and that was with my portrait. And now...'

Louise looked up, she wanted to thank Gaston for listening ... but the day had finally taken its toll. His head had sunk forward, his forehead was resting on his hands; he was fast asleep.

CHAPTER 5

The Call of Home

It was dark when Colette woke on the morning following Gaston's drunken departure. At fourteen, she was sensitive to that slight tension, that feeling of anticipation that comes before the first cock begins to crow. She had gone to bed feeling miserable and defeated, Gaston's broken promise seeming to highlight just how irrelevant she was to this family. Now she felt only anger. New energy began to flow through her. She was tired of this house, tired of being preserved by Madame as a living ghost of her mother. She found herself sitting up in bed. Charity – that was what Madame was offering – and she, Colette, would not accept charity! Whatever about dropping the aristocratic 'de' from her name, she would not be a subject of charity! She swung her feet onto the floor. She would go away from here and find work as a servant, or even work in the fields.

But where could she go? She sat on the edge of her bed. Obviously, the village was out of the question. Her family had had friends, but they had mostly fled or were dead. What about relations? None alive that she knew of. Then, almost reluctantly, she remembered her old home. She had locked it away in a hidden corner of her mind, but now she could see it: the tumbling roofs and garrets of the old chateau. She had hated it once, seeing it as one vast prison, but now its seedy grandeur called to her. She knew every room, every outhouse and every turret. The property had been confiscated by the Revolution but she would find a way in, and there were people there who had known her – men on the farm, her old nurse – they would see that she got food until she found some means of supporting herself.

A cock crowed somewhere in the distance. She knew the winery well enough by now to be able to slip out without being seen or heard. She must be dressed and far away before the family stirred. Her teeth chattered with the cold, or perhaps with nervousness, as she pulled on her clothes. She added several extra layers to save her having to carry a bundle, which would only attract attention. She slipped the small amount of money she possessed into her pocket, but left the few jewels her mother had bequeathed her in their box on the dressing table. Madame would look after them. Colette felt bitter about those jewels; Maman could have saved herself by selling them for food, instead of preserving them as a dowry for Colette. When she was established in her new life she would come back and thank Madame; she had no wish to appear ungrateful.

It was Lucien, on his way back from one of his longer night-time forays, who saw Colette walking purposefully along the road, about a mile south of the village. He didn't recognise her at first, her slender figure bulked out by the extra clothes. But her pale face attracted his attention; this was no country lass. Over time Lucien had evolved an invariable policy with girls that he might meet; and that was to smile at them all. If they were pretty, he argued, it pleased him, and if they were not, surely it would please them. Colette kept her head down demurely as the young man approached, but there was something about his walk that was familiar, it certainly didn't seem threatening. She looked up, and found herself bathed in one of Lucien's most radiant smiles. Disarmed, she smiled back, and then in a pace or two they were past each other. It was only then that Colette realised who the young man was. She ducked her head into her shoulders and hurried on. He must have recognised her, why else had he smiled? He'd tell everyone; she must hurry. She heard him turn, but if he was about to call after her, he thought better of it. What she didn't know was that Lucien would have no wish to advertise his night-time wanderings by telling where he'd seen her.

Colette's departure from the winery was not noticed as early as it might have been. The alarms and excitements of the previous day had knocked them all out of routine. Madame had seen that Colette was upset about something the night before, but didn't associate this with her son. She assumed it had been caused by the confrontation with the mob. Poor child, God knew what associations that might have brought to mind. It was mid-morning, therefore, before, out of kindness, she sent Margot up to Colette's room with a cup of coffee, and was nonplussed when she heard that Colette was not there. Perhaps Monsieur Morteau would know, but he had gone down to talk to Brouchard at the mill. Not having been witness to Margot's confrontation with Lucien the day before, she couldn't understand why Margot made such a fuss about taking a message to the mill. Eventually Margot went off, carrying some eggs for Madame Brouchard, by way of a reason for going.

Lucien saw Margot coming from a distance and stepped back into the cavernous dark of the grain-hoist above the door to watch her approach. She had a basket, so she must have some errand to do with the family below. As he had hoped, she didn't raise her eyes. He felt an unaccustomed pang of conscience. He thought of Bernadette – she of the two handprints – but that wasn't his fault. All he had done was smile at her, and if he hadn't held her she might have fallen over backwards. He sighed; his recent night-time expedition had been a disappointment, perhaps he should settle down. He watched Margot leave, her backside swinging defiantly, with something more than regret. She didn't look back. He had to find out why she had called, so he took a fistful of the flour flowing from under the spinning millstone and backed down the ladder to talk about it with his employer. When he opened the door of the office he saw that M. Morteau from the winery was there.

'I must go at once,' the vigneron was saying. 'Why on earth would the girl leave us? Do you think it was anything to do with the trouble yesterday? Perhaps she is still on the farm; she sometimes goes out to pick mulberries, I will look there.'

Lucien stepped aside to let M. Morteau leave. He guessed who they were talking about, but if he told M. Morteau what he had seen, news of his wandering would be up at the winery before he could say 'knife'. And that would be the last he'd see of Margot.

'I don't understand you, Lucien. Why didn't you tell me before, when M. Morteau was here? And what the devil were you doing on that road at six in the morning?' M. Brouchard looked angrily at his employee and saw that he was actually blushing under his dusting of flour. The older man groaned, 'No, no, please don't tell me, I don't want to know.' He ran his hands through his hair, raising a cloud of white about his head. 'Where could she be going?'

'Where is her old home?' Lucien asked. Monsieur Brouchard looked up, impressed. The lad was showing more intelligence than he expected. He wondered if he dare tell Lucien who young Colette was?

'Now, understand Lucien, what I am about to tell you is a secret, one that could endanger that child's life if it ever got out. She is one of the de Valenods ... the last of them, I suspect. You've probably seen their chateau; it's about fifteen miles from here, in the direction in which you saw her walking. I think you may well be right – she is heading home.'

'But hasn't the chateau been–'

'Yes, but the question is, does the girl know?' M. Brouchard leaned back in his high chair and looked at the ceiling, the draped and dusty cobwebs hung above him as if they had been caught in an early frost. He knew very little about this girl; the Morteaus had, understandably, kept quiet about her presence. He wondered what would it be like for her up there? Madame Morteau had no daughter of her own; she would like having a girl in the house, but what status would she have: aristocrat or Cinderella? Then there was young Gaston; he had seen how the child looked at him after he had sung his song yesterday. He shook himself. There was no point in speculating.

'Lucien, go and harness the horse, she can clip on at a good pace, and I daresay the girl is not that used to walking; I will catch up with her soon enough.'

'I'll go!' Lucien said eagerly, suddenly seeing himself in the role of the saviour of a maiden in distress.

'No, Lucien! I would as soon send a wolf to rescue a lamb. But I will take the almost equal risk of leaving you in charge of the mill till I get back.'

Colette shaded her eyes and looked ahead to where the road climbed steeply. The midday sun beat down on the top of her head and set the road a-shimmer. Oh, if only she had brought a hat. She singled out a clump of brilliant red poppies as her next rest stop and tried to measure the distance to that spot. Surely this would be the last rest she'd need before she topped the rise and looked down on her old home. Already the view was laid out in her mind: the road dipping down into the green valley, the glint of the river as it curved around the home pasture, and then the lawns rising to the warm glow of the sandstone walls and turrets of the chateau. As she walked she had been reviving all the nice associations she could conjure up from a lonely childhood there. But she mustn't take her eyes from the poppies, if she did the road would pitch and sway again. The sun seemed to be boring through the top of her skull. The extra clothes she had put on in the morning had been removed one by one and were now an awkward bundle under her arm. Finally she reached the poppies and their blowsy heads filled her whole vision as she sank down in front of them. She felt the sharp prickles from the roadside verge under her hands, angled stones were pressing on her thigh. She would rest for a little while … just a little while.

She woke with a start. In the distance she could hear a cart coming up the hill behind her. She felt refreshed from her sleep but when she tried to move, her whole body pro-tested in pain. She might be able to beg a ride on the cart, but first she was determined to get to the top of the hill. That had been her mission – to capture her first view of home by herself, on her own. She heaved herself to her feet, grabbed her bundle, and set off for the crest. Her feet felt like burning coals.

Jean Brouchard had been worried that he had seen no sign of the girl; could she really have walked so far? Had he missed her? Perhaps she had got a ride from someone? He had driven hard, his horse was tired, and now there was a clink from a loose shoe on the off side. Better to let it set its own pace. If he remembered rightly, they would see the de Valenod estate from the top of the hill.

But the next minute Jean was on his feet in the cart, slapping the reins down on the horse's rump, 'Giddup!' he urged. A small figure had detached itself from the roadside verge. Surely that was she? He screwed up his eyes and groaned as he saw her stumble and sway to regain her balance. If only he could reach her before she got to the top of the hill. The cart bounced jerkily as the horse broke into a trot, but soon slowed to a steady plod again. Perhaps he should shout? No, that might just frighten the girl. He watched in despair as she climbed to the crest of the hill.

She had made it, and she had beaten the cart to the top. This was the moment Colette had been waiting for, a moment to be savoured. She looked down into the valley ahead. She shook her head. Had she made some mistake? She searched the landscape for familiar landmarks. There was the valley, the river; even the home pasture seemed to be right, but where …? At last her eyes took in what her heart was denying. Yes, the chateau was there – one of its turrets still stood – but it, and all else, was no more now than a burnt out blackened hulk. Then darkness closed over her.

Jean watched the small figure as she approached the sky-line; he saw her stop to survey the view, and then he saw her drop where she stood, like a shot bird. 'Damn them!' he swore, urging his horse into a reluctant trot again, 'Why didn't they tell her?'

He picked the girl up carefully, so light after the sacks of grain he handled daily, and carried her to where he had drawn the cart up in the shade of some hazel bushes. He had to get her away from that dreadful view of her ruined home. He rested her head on the bundle of clothes and fanned at her with his hat. The air stirred the dark swirl of hair that framed her unconscious face. For all that she had lived a life of privilege, she was a plucky little creature. The blood was returning, flushing her cheeks; she had caught the sun and the extra colour became her. He smiled as he saw her eyelids flicker.

Colette opened her eyes to a face that smiled down on her. It was vaguely familiar; a countryman's face, lined by not too many years, fine wrinkles radiating from his eyes. It was the sort of face that in her previous life she would have identified as belonging to 'them' rather than 'us'. But that had all changed, hadn't it? She had crossed that divide ... she tried to remember why. It had something to do with the hill. Her eyes opened wide in shock.

'It's gone, isn't it? The chateau ... my home?' Her rescuer looked concerned, though the smile remained about his eyes. His large hand rhythmically swept a battered hat to and fro above her head.

'Yes, I'm afraid it was burned to the ground a month ago.'

'I didn't know ... nobody said. Was anyone hurt?'

'No, it was empty, the servants and the workers had all gone.'

'I'm glad of that at least. I wanted to go back there, you know.'

'We guessed that; that is why I came after you.'

'After me?'

'Yes, I'm Jean Brouchard … from the mill. You were missed, and my mill-hand said he had seen you on the road. I'm sorry about …' Colette looked up at the sky; the inferno that had been the sun was gone now. She felt curiously relaxed, as if a burden had been lifted from her. 'Don't be sorry. I was trying to go back, but it's not possible, is it? I don't belong there any more; I don't belong anywhere now.' She wanted to close her eyes and go on lying there, suspended between her past and her future. But she'd have to decide what to do. 'I'm sorry, I'm keeping you, I'll be all right now.'

'But I'm here to take you …' he paused, he wanted it to be her choice, 'to take you wherever you want to go.'

Colette absorbed this. Until this morning it had always been other people, or circumstances, that had decided her life. Since this morning she had taken her life in her own hands, so her decision was really quite easy:

'I will go home, ' she said.

'And where is home?'

'To Monsieur and Madame Morteau, if they will have me; that is my home now.' She managed to sit up. It was only when she tried to stand that she realised that her feet could take no more. Jean Brouchard, gentle giant that he was, lifted her up and sat her on the board that spanned the front of the cart, padding her around with empty grain sacks. It would be a slow journey, he explained, his horse had lost a shoe and they would have to stop at a smithy on the way home.

Colette slept while the smith worked, waking only when they started out again. The clip-clop of shod hooves on the road was hypnotic, and the fading light threw a protective shield about them. The evening scents of crushed thyme and brushed lavender soothed the air. Little by little, Colette found herself talking about her life in the chateau, and then her life since she had come to live with the Morteaus. She found words for things that, till then, had been no more than feelings: how Madame seemed to be preserving her for a life that meant nothing to Colette. How she seemed to have no function and no position in the family. She even told the miller how jealous she was of Margot's freedom. When Jean Brouchard heard how Margot had detected Lucien's philandering by seeing his two handprints on Bernadette's back, the miller roared with laughter.

'No more than he deserves!' he chuckled, as he got down to light a lantern which he hung on the side of the cart.

Lamps lit up the winery too when Jean turned his weary horse into the yard. Madame, hearing hooves, appeared in a rush.

'Shhhh,' Jean lifted a finger to his lips. Colette was fast asleep, nestling in the crook between his arm and his shoulder.

In some other part of the house, Madame and Margot were tending a mildly protesting Colette. No questions were being asked. In Paul Morteau's study, Jean Brouchard held his glass up to the light of the candle and looked appreciatively at the slightly tawny red of the fine old vintage his friend had opened for him. It was time for him to go. He had told nothing that would betray Colette's confidences to him, but there were things that had to be said on her behalf, and a suggestion or two to be made.

'Try it, Paul,' he said, 'and if Madame objects to her helping you in the vineyards on account of her complexion, tell her that it is Colette's pallor that singles her out as an enemy of the Revolution. Get her out into the fields. Let her mix with the village folk and let her become one of us, for her own safety. I tell you, if anyone in the village speaks out against her, they will have me to contend with. Come on, Paul, I'm worn out; drink her health, and if you don't want her in the vineyards, send her down to me at the mill and I'll look after her.'

CHAPTER 6

Crossing The Rhine

Gaston sat on his horse on the high levee looking out over the frozen Rhine. A warm wind blew in from the west. Crossing here was a risk but it would save two days' march and unknown troubles at the nearest bridge. Cracks and groans from the tired ice warned of its imminent break up. Gaston winced as a report like a cannon came from where the men were filing out onto the ice. Far across the wide expanse he could see the diminishing figures of Pierre and Marcel walking beside their horses at the head of line of hussars, each spaced precisely twenty-five paces apart on the ice.

'You shouldn't have let them go.' Louise's voice echoed exactly what he had been feeling deep in his mind. Gaston could still be alarmed by her unexpected appearances. There had been several days' delay in their departure from Maarssen and, while he was waiting for the order to proceed, Gaston had had plenty of time to observe Louise's portrait on its stand in his room. When he woke after hearing her tragic story she was gone; there was just the painting propped up on his bed. At first he was uneasy and tried to avoid looking at it; then, as a sort of test, he had stood in front of the picture, a self-mocking smile on his face, and made a conscious effort get the girl to appear again, only to end up doubting his sanity when nothing happened. Then, when he least expected it, catching sight of her portrait out of the corner of his eye perhaps, he would feel his energy flow out to her in sudden empathy, and her presence would suffuse the room. He would hear her voice behind him, and when he turned, there she would be, laughing at him, as real and tangible to him as if she were alive.

'Mademoiselle Louise,' he said after one of her visits. 'Why is it that your appearances do not frighten me, or have me banging my head against the wall, demanding a strait-jacket and a place in a lunatic asylum?'

'I hadn't thought about it; I suppose they *could* be frightening. So how *do* they make you feel?'

'I just feel normal. Although I am still surprised when you appear, at the same time it seems the most natural thing in the world. But no one would believe me if I told them about you, would they? And I sometimes wonder where you are, really – here, or in your picture, or in my head?'

'It is difficult to explain. To begin with it never occurred to me that I could appear to anyone. I was aware of Pieter moving about me and working on my portrait and I just delighted in his presence. The first time I actually appeared was to Master Haitink, when he was sick. I had felt him calling and calling me but I didn't know that I could go to him. Then one day it just happened, and I was the one who was astonished. All he did was look me up and down and say, "So there you are, and about time too." I think he wasn't surprised because he believed in me; after all, he had painted me to live in the minds of others. And now you are recreating me as he saw me: argumentative maybe, a nuisance sometimes, but not frightening.'

At first they had both been worried that Raoul or one of the boys might see her. Gaston's quarters were an open house to his men; they came and went for orders all the time. But none of them showed any sign of seeing Louise.

When at last the order had come to proceed, Gaston was as happy as a sand boy. On the first morning's ride he had gazed about the frozen landscape and sniffed at the thaw in the air, thinking how much Louise would enjoy being able to see this. She was travelling with them, of course, her portrait securely strapped to one of the remounts. He imagined her riding out here with him, the billowing silk of her green dress causing her all kinds of problems. At that moment Pierre trotted up to ask for permission to ride ahead, so that the baker in the next village could have bread ready for the troop when they arrived. Gaston watched him canter off, a splash of youthful colour, and thought how Louise would look in the boy's uniform. The first intimation he had that she had joined him was the sudden feeling of companionship that he associated with her. Then he heard her voice.

'What have you done to me, Gaston?' Then a surprised laugh. 'But I like it!'

Gaston turned and nearly unseated himself in surprise. There she was, riding, just as he had imagined her, looking delighted with herself as she examined the hussar outfit he had thought up for her. Gaston stammered.

'I … I wanted to share this with you.'

'Oh, Gaston, thank you. Thank you for the uniform, and thank you for calling me.' Her eyes were dancing. 'Where are we going?'

'We are going south. We are to escort General Daendels's courier to Paris. But the thaw is coming and I want to get across the Rhine while it is still frozen. It's touch and go.'

'Do let me ride with you, Gaston, please. I promise I will keep out of your way. Oh, if only the Master could see me now; when I think of the trouble he took with my green dress!' A buffet of warm wind plucked at her shako. She put up her hand to steady it and looked around, drinking in the familiar Dutch landscape.

'Forgive me, Louise, but we must press on. I want to be at the Rhine by first light tomorrow before the sun gets to work.' Gaston turned and roared: 'Marcel, *dépêchez-vous!*'

Now, in the early morning light, Gaston watched as the line of men leading their horses filed out on to the ice.

'Look, they've stopped,' Louise said. The line had halted as one. That was good discipline. It could be a disaster if they all crowded forward, overloading the ice at any one point. Gaston could see the boys casting left and right. Then the whole column started moving again, this time snaking upstream away from where one of the boys – Pierre, he thought – stood guard.

'There must be a crack there.' said Gaston, 'He's seeing that it isn't spreading as they pass. Good thinking.' The head of the line was now approaching the opposite bank. 'I'm going down to see the carriage safely on to the ice.' He urged his horse forward, leaning back in the saddle as the path plunged down through the broken trees lining the levee. The freeze had come while the river was in flood. When the level of the water under the ice had dropped, the ice that was still clinging to the trees had torn at the branches, stripping them off at the trunks. They had chosen to cross at a point where a sloping slab of solid ice led out onto the frozen river surface, and had covered this with branches and straw to give the wheels a better purchase. The soldiers were just easing the adjutant's carriage down the slope, holding it back with ropes. The officer whose privilege it was to bring the official news of the campaign's success to Paris was watching the proceedings with interest. Gaston saluted. The courier, Captain Sorel, was a handsome man, dressed in black knee-length boots, white trousers, a cutaway coat of French blue and a red waistcoat.

'Isn't he beautiful?' whispered Louise. Gaston ignored her.

'Will you walk, sir?'

'Should I? Perhaps as captain I should go down with my ship.' The man laughed. 'All the same, I think I will go on foot. If I walk ahead of the carriage, I can at least run in the right direction if it breaks through. Well done, Lieutenant, it looks to have been a neat operation.'

The carriage rolled off on to the ice. There were just some remounts and pack animals to follow. Gaston congratulated the dispatchers. He could see the glitter from the men and harness as they moved up the far levee, so he rode out onto the river with a lighter heart. If the ice could take the weight of the carriage, it could take him on his horse. The warm wind blowing over the cold ice was strangely exhilarating. He stood in his stirrups, gazing in awe up and down the sweep of the mighty river. It seemed mysterious and wonderful that this water, that had begun its journey in the Alps, was even now flowing under his horse's hooves. Where was Louise? He wanted to share the moment with her. He looked downstream; there she was, riding her horse as only a girl fortified by his own imagination could ride. She looked back at him and laughed, then she pulled off the shako and shook out her hair.

'So this is the Rhine?' she called, her face lit up with excitement. 'And I'm to cross it!'

After her sheltered life in the walled town of Delft, Louise found the world of straining horses and swearing men both exhilarating and exhausting. They had been on the road for several days now, fighting their way at first through melting snow and then through mud so thick that it frequently reached to the rider's stirrups. Without the carriage they could have made twenty miles in a day, but protocol demanded that the news be brought to Paris in proper style. Most of the time Gaston was too preoccupied or exhausted to give Louise much thought. She, on the other hand, wanted to see everything and got him to promise that he would think of her when there was anything interesting for her to see. Then she could ride beside him until some distraction would pluck his thoughts away from her and she would be obliged to fade back into the picture until the crisis was over. Louise was delighted with Gaston's company. Since that one time after his fever when he had shouted at her, he had never raised his voice again. He was courteous and kind, and seemed genuinely to like having her to talk to. Then there came an incident that made her realise that there was another side to Gaston.

The pattern of their advance was always the same. Five men from the troop would ride ahead, reconnoitring the road and clearing it of all traffic. Usually it was enough for oncoming carts and carriages to pull off to one side, but if the road was narrow, or the carters uncooperative, the soldiers had little compunction about forcing obstructing vehicles off the road. One day, Gaston and Louise were riding at the rear of the column, avoiding the mud by walking their horses through the open fields beside the road. A cart, piled high with firewood, sagged over to one side, its wheels mired to the hubs in the ditch. Suddenly, as if out of the earth, the driver materialised, saw Gaston, and let out a stream of invective.

'You bastards, you bloody French bastards. Will you look where my f...ing cart is? How am I going to get out of here? Give me the Austrians any time, even the f...ing Spaniards. Do you know what is good about them? They've bloody gone away, and the sooner you bloody go away the f...ing better.'

Louise gazed down into the coarse face of the peasant. His blackened teeth were gapped and, in his fury, spittle trickled through the stubble of his Friday beard – he would shave once a week on Sunday and come to church nicked and bleeding. Louise realised that Gaston could only guess at what the man was saying although the meaning was obvious enough. But the south Dutch patois, foul-mouthed though it was, stirred Louise's patriotism.

'How is he going to get out?' she asked.

'He was in the way,' Gaston growled, turning away from the man in disgust.

'That's not what I asked. How is he going to get out?'

'That's his problem, *c'est la vie.*' Gaston was moving forward, prepared to leave the man behind.

Louise was annoyed. She urged her horse past him and wheeled across his line.

'Gaston Morteau, you may not understand what this man is saying, but I do. He is cursing you – the French – as in my day he would have cursed the Spanish, and since then apparently the Austrians. He's a peasant! Where is your noble revolution? Do you leave the people you are supposed to have liberated rotting in the ditch?'

Gaston shook his head and she could feel him trying to clear her image from his mind, but she resisted.

'Get out of my way, or I will ride through you!'

'You could try. But that doesn't sound like the noble lieutenant who fished me out of a canal.'

'I did that for the boys, as an example,' Gaston replied shortly.

Louise didn't move, and finally he shrugged in a resigned way. 'All right, *Mademoiselle*, what am I supposed to do?'

'Call Pierre. Look, he's waiting for the carriage to move forward. There are spare horses ... remounts you called them. Get him to organise your men to pull the cart out, and France will have one less enemy in the Netherlands.'

'I will be a laughing stock.'

'No. No more, Lieutenant, than you were when you dived into a canal to rescue a mere picture.'

'I should have let you drown!' Gaston said, with more conviction than Louise would have liked.

'Well, do this for Pierre then, *as an example!*'

Gaston shrugged, but he cupped his hands and called out to Pierre, *'Ici! Viens!* Cadet Colbert.'

The Pont de Chasse

'Never interfere again!' Gaston was furious; he had heard Marcel scoffing at Pierre over the incident of the cart. 'You made me look foolish, and Pierre too. What will the soldiers think: that we are a charity?' Gaston was lodged in a small hotel on the outskirts of Brussels. Louise was refusing to appear, so he was addressing the darkness where her portrait stood at the end of his bed. 'Never...' he began again ... but at that moment there was a knock on the door. He strode across the room and snatched it open. A maid stood there holding a warming pan. She bobbed a curtsey and walked in.

'I thought you had someone with you, sir,' she said, looking around. Gaston, recovering from his surprise, rose to his full height.

'*Au contraire*, Mademoiselle, alas, I'm alone ... but do I have to be?' With a glance towards the portrait, he swept his moustaches and aimed a kiss at the girl's cheek. The maid dodged him with a laugh and plunged the pan of hot coals into his bed. She worked it deftly into the four corners of the bed and then drew it slowly up the middle. When she turned, he barred her way and raised his shoulders pleadingly: 'Mademoiselle, you cannot leave me now ... and look!' he glanced innocently towards the bed. 'You have started a fire.' The girl turned back involuntarily.

'Where?'

'Why here, my princess, the fire is in my heart!' He had his arms held out, ready for her. For a second Louise thought the maid was going to succumb, but then, just when she seemed to be about melt into Gaston's embrace, she gave a sharp thrust of the hot warming pan to his stomach and was out of the door with another laugh before he could recover.

'Do you always behave like that?' Louise said, appearing beside her portrait and trying to sound disapproving as Gaston dusted the ashes from his trousers.

'*Mais oui!* Why not? She is pretty. Also it is expected of me.'

'Like driving peasants' carts into ditches?'

'Don't start that again!' He banged the table. Then realising that he had shouted, he put his head in his hands. 'Look what you are doing to me, Mademoiselle Louise; my reputation will be ruined. First there is Pierre laughing behind my back, then I fail to get my arms around the prettiest girl in Brussels, and now I am talking to myself.'

'Shouting at *me* actually,' said Louise. 'Would you like me to go again?'

'Yes, go away. Life with a soldier is clearly not for you.'

'Soldier?' Louise hadn't meant it to sound scornful, but that was how it came out.

'What do you think I am, then?' Gaston blazed. 'A philanthropist with a mission to rescue carts from ditches! You are damaging my pride… my dignity. Look at me, woman,' he said, and he hit his chest with his fist. 'I am a lieutenant of the Hussars of Auxerre, a soldier of France. I am not just moustaches and swagger, I have my honour, and inside this chest beats a heart of steel. You know nothing of the soldier in action; when I draw my sword it is *pour la France, la gloire!*

Louise looked around, there was little furnishing in the room apart from a chair, turned aside from the fire, and a foot-stool for the tired traveller. Louise went to the stool and sat down.

'Sit, Gaston, I want you to tell me about the engagement at the Pont de Chasse. I heard it was a great fight. Perhaps I will understand then what it means to be a soldier.'

Gaston started towards the chair, and then hesitated. 'How did you hear about the Pont de Chasse?' he asked.

'You were talking to Raoul, but I'm afraid you were rather drunk.'

'Raoul doesn't know what happened.'

'But you do; you were there. Take me there, too,' she said.

'Take you there?' Gaston repeated. 'But it happened a year and a half ago. How can I take you there?'

'It's something my father used to do, from when I was quite little. Whenever he came back from his journeys I would ask him to tell me all about the places he'd been to, all the things he had done and seen. I would say: "Take me there," then I would hold his hand, and he would remember, and tell the story for me, and it would feel as if I was actually there.' Without thinking, she held out her hand, but Gaston thrust his hands into his pockets. When he began, it was to address the floor.

'It sounds like a lot of nonsense to me, but if it will stop you meddling in my affairs it will be worth it.'

Louise rested her hands in her lap, closed her eyes, and tried to focus her mind on Gaston's. He padded up and down the room a few times. She could feel him getting ready, like an actor preparing for a performance. When he began to speak the room faded, and Gaston's voice became an echo in some other part of her mind. She was with him now, riding unseen, as she had so often ridden with him over the past weeks. It was early morning and she was watching a small troop of hussars filing through the trees towards a forest's edge.

The smell of stirred beech leaves mixed with the scent of meadow grass rising from the sloping fields below. Gaston – his moustaches a mere promise of their present glory – looked ridiculously young. She saw him hold up his hand. The troop halted as one, and Gaston rode out into the sunlight that flooded the forest shore. Louise urged her horse forward so that she could watch. Below them, broad meadows swept down to where a river, silver in the morning sun, snaked through the grass. Beyond the river was a modest chateau, and in front of the chateau arched a bridge. A hunting horn began to toot from the chateau walls. Louise could see figures pointing up at them in alarm. She could hear the thud of hooves as the horses moved out of the forest behind them. They blew and shook their heads in the pollen-laden air. A group of peasants was frantically manoeuvring a hay-wain on to the bridge. Men with scythes and pitchforks were converging on it from the chateau and the nearby cottages. As she watched the scene unfold she could hear Gaston reciting his account of the encounter as he remembered it.

'It was the second year of the Republic, Floréal – the month of Blossom – or May as it used to be called,' his voice intoned. 'Our mission was of the utmost importance. That day I was in command of my first patrol, a mere sub-lieutenant, but the whole regiment was depending on our success. I rode forward from the darkness of the forest. Below was the bridge and I realised that I was looking at the only access to the chateau. Perhaps the sun had flashed on my accoutrements, as there wasn't an unpolished piece of metal about me; at any rate a horn started to blow a frantic warning from the chateau walls. I realised at once that we had happened on a nest of vipers, a force of Royalists resistant to the Republic. Here at last was an opportunity to prove myself in battle. I called my men forward and lined them up in full view along the edge of the forest. A substantial force was fast gathering at the bridge. I could see the sun flashing on their weapons. If we didn't act quickly they would succeed in barricading the bridge against us. We were outnumbered, of course, but that was a challenge, not a deterrent. I encouraged my men; now was a chance to strike a blow for the Republic. Oh, Mademoiselle Louise, the excitement ...' She could indeed hear the thrill in Gaston's voice. 'If you have never been in a cavalry charge, you have never lived, if you have never ridden with the Hussars of Auxerre you can have no idea of heaven. We drew sabres and swept down on them like the wolf on the fold. As we approached we let out a yell that echoed off the chateau walls beyond the bridge.

'Their leader was the one I was after. I singled him out: a big black-visaged Royalist on a mighty horse. We closed; I parried his blow. His horse reared. I saw that he was losing his seat so I threw myself out of my saddle and bore him to the ground. Above me the battle raged. I staggered to my feet. It was over. Their leader lay dead at my feet, and the enemy, seeing their leader slain, fled. We crossed the bridge and the chateau was ours.'

The story was over. Louise sensed that this was the

moment in the re-telling when glasses would have been charged in a toast to the Republic ... But it was taking her some time to return from the field of battle. She had never seen a man slain before, and the sight had shaken her. She looked up. Gaston was standing, still glowing from his account. The firelight flickered on his wind-burnt face, framed by his four braids. This for him was how it had really happened. But it was not the battle that Louise had just seen.

Dare she challenge him? Or would it be kinder to let him continue in his dream? But if she wasn't mistaken, there was a well of unhappiness behind his bravado. She thought of Annie, her old nurse back in Delft, and felt a sudden pang of regret for her – brave little Annie, with her unrelenting Calvinistic truthfulness. And sometimes there was a need for truth.

'So you got your hay,' she said softly.

'Hay? What are you talking about?' Gaston demanded.

'I mean that you were ... what do you call it? ... a foraging party looking for hay for your horses.' She had heard the men talking while they waited for the advance. It was not the glorious spectacle that Gaston had described, but a humble enough troop in their foraging clothes. 'There was really no need to attack the chateau.'

'What absolute nonsense!' Gaston declared, but the bluster was leaking from his voice. Louise was encouraged and at the same time saddened. She watched him as he gradually deflated, and remembered an occasion when she had seen children playing with a ball, a blown up bladder from the butcher's. It had landed on a thorn, and she recalled the children's disappointment as the ball had slowly collapsed.

'You shouldn't talk to Raoul,' he muttered defensively, but all the swagger had gone and his shoulders were slumped.

'Raoul doesn't know that I exist, Gaston. I asked *you* to take me there, to the Pont de Chasse, and that's what you did. You showed it to me as it really was. I saw it all, Gaston: they were peasants with scythes.'

Louise gestured to the chair beside her; Gaston took it cautiously as if uncertain that she could be trusted. Then he took a deep breath, and began to talk. His eyes, turned inward now, were no more than dark smudges on his face, but his voice had its own authority.

'Yes, Louise, we were a foraging party – horses need hay, and we could have got it elsewhere, but there was rebellion in the air. We were in that area to establish order. The men were thinking of fodder, of course, but to have turned our back on resistance of any sort would have just encouraged further resistance.' He put up his hand as if Louise was going to interrupt. 'I heard what you said, and yes, they were "peasants with scythes" but scythes, though they may be good for cutting hay, make very bad weapons. Those peasants were a danger to themselves. You saw how we advanced, with a lot of yelling, head on. If we had wanted to kill them we'd have stopped at a few paces off and used our pistols, and then come out through the smoke with sabres drawn. They wouldn't have known what was happening. No, my idea was to scare them; you saw how they broke and ran.'

'Except for one,' said Louise bitterly.

'Except for one.' Gaston stared at the floor, his eyes retreating deeper and deeper into their sockets. He whispered, 'I loved that man, Louise.'

'You knew him?' Louise was startled.

'For thirty seconds I knew him and I loved him. Would God that I could have that thirty seconds again – wind the clock back – and start over. I will tell you now what I have told no one else. I will tell it to you as it really was.

'As you saw, he stood his ground. I couldn't understand it. His men had fled but he sat there on his horse, as solid as a rock, staring at twenty raised sabres. My men held back; as their officer, it fell to me to tackle this man. I had no pistols that day. If he would not surrender I would have to kill him or he would kill me – the soldier's choice. There comes a point of no return, you see. I slowed to a walk. I shouted to him: "Throw down your sword!" He didn't blink. I spurred my horse and yelled again. I closed on him. I had no choice. At last his sword came up. Thank God, I thought, a fair fight! I was trained for a moment such as this; a wild joy filled me. We closed, but instead of crossing my sword to parry my stroke, he left himself unprotected and prodded at me, just as a student might when fighting epée in fencing school. It was this naivety that caused me to stay my hand; but I was still wide open and it took all my skill to turn his sword. I looked into his face then, amazed – we had been taught to read an enemy's intentions from his face. What I saw in his was fear and valour ... and total perplexity.

'Louise, in that instant the whole complexion of our fight changed. This was no black-visaged warrior. True, he had nearly killed me, but that was in error. What I saw was a sensitive, intelligent face. His clothes were those of a landowner, but not some idle aristocrat; he was burned by the sun. This man surely had been at work in the fields with his peasants.'

Gaston sighed and dropped his head. 'What notion of honour or obligation had brought him out to hold the bridge against a troop of hussars I will never know. I hauled at the reins of my mare – she could turn on a centime. His mount, a common carthorse, was at last showing signs of life, plunging and bucking. I was beside him, holding my sword above my head to keep it out of the way. I realise now he must have thought that this was the *coup de grâce* – the moment when I would cut him down.'

Gaston paused, Louise could hear his knuckles cracking under the pressure he was putting on them. 'He smiled at me, Louise. He smiled apologetically, like someone asking forgiveness for not being able to conclude a game, because right then he needed both hands to control his horse. I, like a fool, was shouting at him to surrender. He nodded, but at that moment his horse bucked and threw him forward. I could see that he was losing his seat. I let go of my reins and reached out with my left hand to steady him.' Gaston's voice dropped. 'My one consolation in all this is that he realised at that moment that I was trying to help him. I remember the look of gratitude in his eyes – a word of thanks on his lips.'

Louise saw a glint on Gaston's cheek and looked away.

'We fell together. As we did so he dropped his sword; he had no loop or sword-knot to prevent it falling, and he fell on top of it. I remember the tearing sound as the blade went through him. You saw me pull a sword from his body? That wasn't mine; it was his. I knelt beside him then and watched the life fade from his eyes.' Gaston could hardly speak. 'Louise, I could have been kneeling at my brother's deathbed.'

A clock ticked laboriously in a corner of the room. The silence grew till it was more than Louise could bear; she had to do something. Without thinking, she turned and knelt in front of Gaston and rested her head and arms on his knees. He stroked her hair.

A hundred and forty years had done nothing to erode

Louise's love for Pieter, the Master's apprentice, who had held her so tight in that dusty room above the Oosterport in her native Delft. But this was a different kind of love. Here, she was a guest of Gaston's mind. It was as if their consciousnesses had merged. But the touch of his hand brought home to her just how much she had missed by her early death and for a moment the loss threatened to overwhelm her. She must grab at every moment: to feel, to touch, to hold and above all understand.

Gaston's hand continued to stroke her hair but his thoughts had wandered to a countryside Louise had never seen before. The image focused and she found herself gazing at a gnarled old tree on a slope above a country road. A girl was sitting under the tree, her eyes fixed on the road below. Louise felt drawn to her, as Gaston obviously was. But here Louise checked. Was she going too far? Had she any right to invade Gaston's private thoughts? Reluctantly she pulled her mind away and the image faded, leaving her with a mixture of longing and a deep sadness. It was some time before either of them spoke.

'Louise,' Gaston asked in a whisper, 'am I really touching you?'

'Yes,' she said softly, 'it shouldn't be possible, should it? Gaston, I'm so sorry … about the Pont de Chasse. I shouldn't have asked.'

'No, I'm glad you did. I feel happier now I have told someone. You see, I'm not a monster, am I, Louise?'

'No, you're not a monster, Gaston.' She slid out from under his hand then, and walked across the room to her picture, the touch of his hand lingering like a memory on her hair.

From Brussels south to Paris the roads were better. They were making good time and Gaston was preoccupied with getting his troop into perfect order for a triumphant entry into Paris. News would, of course, have reached the capital, both of their coming and of their success in Amsterdam, but this was the official confirmation of the diplomatic coup, and the presentation of General Daendels's reports. Louise kept to herself and her portrait remained in its case.

CHAPTER 8

Putting down Roots

Monsieur Morteau waited until Colette's blistered feet had recovered from her long walk, and dark smudges of exhaustion no longer circled her eyes, before putting Jean Brouchard's plan into action. *Take her out with you into the vineyards,* the miller had said, *and teach her about your vines. What Colette needs is sun and air, and above all something to occupy her mind.*

Colette's eyes widened when M. Morteau presented her with a pair of sabots that were suitable for work in the fields.

'Come, my dear,' he said, 'It's time for me to introduce you to my class of '92. They hold great promise, my little grapes. In a week or two it will be their harvest, and we will be too busy to give them the attention they deserve.' As he spoke he watched her face closely. Was that a little flash of interest? Perhaps Brouchard was right.

Colette hurried through her few chores and then asked Madame Morteau if she could go. She anticipated objections, or lamentations about her complexion, but Madame seemed to know about the arrangement and even produced a pretty, wide brimmed hat, trimmed with forget-me-nots, to protect her from the sun. Colette was touched. She kissed her benefactor and managed to whisper, '*Merci, Maman,*' and the words didn't stick on her tongue.

Farm gates opened from the rear of the winery directly on

to the slopes above. Colette could see M. Morteau gazing up at the geometric outlines of vineyard, each field a corduroy of lush green vines. He turned, saw her standing in the gate, and swept his arm in the direction of the fields as if inviting her to enjoy his pleasure and his pride. She felt a little guilty; she had been inclined to think of Gaston's father as an old fuddy duddy, kind-hearted but possibly a bit odd. Now, looking at the regimented beauty of the slopes, she began to revise her opinion. This really was a creation, not just a part of the landscape. The gravelly soil crunched under her feet as she climbed towards him.

Eight men from the village worked all year in the vineyards. At six o'clock each morning they would appear in the yard, stretching and talking among themselves in low voices. Then M. Morteau would come out and give them their tasks for the day. They would disperse up the slopes, or into the cool recesses of the winery and the cellars beneath, as they had been directed. Today they were high on the slopes; she could see their heads above the vines, working in a line, talking no doubt, moving methodically towards the skyline.

'So, you have come, my dear, and with a becoming hat too!' His eyes sparkled. He reached out and lifted a bunch of grapes. 'Now, let me introduce you to … how shall I say,' he lowered his voice, 'to some of my less able pupils.' Colette suppressed a smile; so he really did talk to his vines! 'Here, put your hand under them and feel them through the palm of your hand.'

Colette slid her hand under the bunch. 'You see, even without squeezing you can tell that they are still hard. Poor dears, they are deprived of light down here, but used in moderation, they have their place in our wine. They give it life, zest if you like.' He winked at Colette and then raised his voice: 'Do you hear that, you dunderheads, you may not be the brightest, but life would be dull without you.' This time Colette had to laugh as she imagined rows of brightened faces looking up. 'That should keep them happy,' he concluded. Colette, bemused but delighted, was inclined to agree.

As they climbed the slopes, M. Morteau continued to address her and his vines without much distinction between the two, but Colette soon realised that there were lessons hidden behind his seemingly casual talk. She learned how the angle to the sun and height of the slope determined the hours of sunlight the grapes enjoyed. He would pick up handfuls of soil so that they could compare the changing colours reflecting the strata underneath.

To begin with, all the vines looked identical to Colette. M. Morteau had nicknames for them, but for now he told her their formal names: Fromenteau, Pinot Noir, Chardonnay, words that seemed to roll in the mouth. When they approached the line of workers the men stood back respectfully, but when M. Morteau spoke with them they talked easily, pointing out damaged plants or stakes; a curled leaf absorbed them for some minutes.

'What are they doing?' Colette asked when they had climbed on further.

'Oh, they are de-shading the bunches. For the last weeks before picking, every grape must get as much sun as possible, so they are removing any leaves that are shading the fruit. Now, up here we are in the scholarship class. The sweeter the fruit, the stronger the wine and the better it will last. Here, hold a bunch like you did before.' The grapes felt warm, almost sensuous in her palm, straining to burst their skins. 'Now we will taste. First we nip the skin with our teeth, because this is where the colour and the first flavours lie. You have heard a bell being struck?' Colette nodded, 'Well, this is the moment when the clapper strikes.' Colette nipped and noticed the small explosion of tastes on her tongue. 'Now, take in the flesh and move it around in your mouth; notice how your tongue and mouth taste different things in different parts. What you are tasting now are longer flavours; in our wine these will linger like the dying tones of our bell. We will pick a bunch and take them down to Maman.'

That evening, when the last bell rang from the church, Colette listened to the note until it faded to nothing. She thought about Gaston without rancour for the first time. Perhaps he *had* to go away for a while and wear his lovely uniform. But she was here, and if M. Morteau would let her, she would learn all she could about the vineyards. She would do this for Gaston. And even if he came home with a beautiful wife on his arm, she would still have a place here; it would be enough just to be near him.

Colette's introduction to the work of the winery was to be a baptism of fire. In two weeks the pickers arrived and the vintage was upon them. How the migrant workers knew when to sweep down on Les Clos du Bois, she did not know, but quite suddenly the yard was full of men and women, tough as the vines themselves, and as black from the sun as the grapes that were waiting for them. There were demands for water, bedding, bread, oil, and all in vast quantities. Colette was overwhelmed; how could Maman, Margot and herself manage? But she hadn't reckoned with the counter invasion that took place as the villagers poured in, pushing her politely aside and taking over the greater part of running the house. The baker's oven never cooled. As soon as the bread was baked and stacked to cool, the butcher appeared with joints of mutton and goat that were thrust into the oven to cook in the declining heat. A huge cauldron mounted on three stones stood in the yard, simmering over a low fire, continually charged with beans, barley, onions, cloves of garlic, herbs and the chopped up smaller cuts of meat, even bones. Someone had to keep stirring with a long paddle to stop it sticking. Just to smell it made one hungry.

Colette found that she was the only person who did not have a special task, but her very idleness gave her the role she needed; she became everyone's messenger. At one minute she would be down at the mill shouting into M. Brouchard's ear that a sack of barley was needed. Next she would be telling M. Morteau, up with the pickers, that the light winepress had broken. Then there would be a plea for water from the pickers. If she didn't know who to go to, she found out, and if she didn't know what the message she had been given meant, she transmitted it faithfully and asked questions later. Soon she knew the names of all the key players in the drama, and even knew intimate details of machines that she had never heard of before.

To begin with, the village workers kept an eye on her to see that she didn't have any trouble from the migrants, who were not above making a pass at any girl if they could. They soon noticed however that she could look after herself; she could be quite like Madame Morteau if she chose.

The grapes came into the yard in purple torrents, but up on the slopes they were being treated with reverential respect. Colette was surprised to come across a pile of discarded grapes that looked to her like the pick of the crop. 'Why throw these out?' she asked the foreman who was supervising the work. 'They look perfect to me.'

'They are the aristocrats, Mademoiselle, so fat they've split their skins.' He laughed. Then dropped his head in embarrassment. 'Pardon, Mademoiselle,' he said. 'No offence.'

As she trudged down the hill, Colette thought about his remark and his embarrassment. So, for all the family's efforts at concealment, the villagers knew about her aristocratic origins. What pleased her, though, was that he had forgotten it. She was becoming accepted. She was singing to herself when she reached the yard.

The frenetic activity didn't stop at sundown. Torches and lanterns were lit, a motley of instruments: oboes, pipes, drums and stringed instruments of various shapes appeared from nowhere and were tuned. Both migrants and villagers then took off their shoes, rolled up their trousers and skirts, and climbed into the shallow foot-press, stamping down the piled grapes with their feet. The music started, and with arms linked over their shoulders, they began to tread the grapes, slowly rotating to the wild skirl of the music. The mush would get more and more liquid as the grapes were broken open by the pressure of their feet. 'It's a gentle way of extracting the juice,' M. Morteau told Colette. 'Why don't you join them? It will be soothing for your feet.' And Colette joined in, to the delight of the workers, and felt the grapes popping between her toes. One by one the treaders would drop out and sit, purple legged, drinking their ration of wine while others took their place in the press. Their energy seemed unbounded. When she mentioned this to one of the village workers he laughed and said that the migrants fought for the privilege of coming to Les Clos du Bois because they were better fed and looked after here than anywhere.

The kitchen was reserved primarily for the family, full-time workers and the more senior village folk who had come to help. They sat shoulder to shoulder about the great table, silently addressing the urgent matter of food. The crude plenty of the yard was augmented with roast meat and fowl and the wine was stronger than that which M. Morteau allowed to flow outside. Often the locals would sing – peasant songs with haunting melodies. Occasionally a gypsy violinist would be invited into the kitchen and Colette would feel her feet tapping involuntarily under the table. If only Gaston could have stayed, instead of rushing off before the harvest, her happiness would have been complete.

Like the vines she now tended, Colette put down roots and grew. Madame might still shake her head over her darkening complexion but M. Morteau watched her looks ripen, and he nurtured her like his vines, encouraging her to respond to the soil and the right mixture of sun and air. She was a ready pupil as, little by little, he followed Jean Brouchard's advice and introduced her to the secrets of his trade, telling her his stories, and letting her taste his vintages until they lived for her as they lived for him.

Cadet Morteau had been gone from the winery for almost a year before he was granted home leave. During that time he had been drilled, shouted at, punished for minor misdemeanours, had shot pistols till his ears rang, slashed and thrust at both his comrades and at straw dummies, and had ridden until he was so saddle sore he could neither sit nor walk. He had had no time to think of home, and if he had thought of girls it had got no further than sideways glances at the handkerchief-waving pretties who loved all hussars as long as they were safely on horseback. There had, of course been clumsy passes at barmaids who knew how to handle cadets better than the cadets did their horses. He had been working on his moustache, shaving it so that it appeared to droop down each side of his mouth. His hair was braided into plaits fore and aft of his ears.

Now he would have a month with his family before he had to return to barracks to sit his sub-lieutenant's exam. He was looking forward to being part of the grape harvest again; last year was the first one he had missed. Gaston reined in his horse at his favourite approach to Les Clos du Bois, a spot overlooking his father's vineyards, and scanned the green order below. As he urged his horse down the bank to the first line of vines, he rather wished that someone could see him descending, gracefully welded to his saddle. At that moment a girl in peasant dress stood up from between the rows and watched him riding down towards her.

'Welcome home, Gaston.' This wasn't quite what he expected, a village girl would not normally address him as Gaston – other than behind a haystack – but he was prepared to be gracious. Then he noticed the girl's hat, trimmed with little blue flowers, hardly peasant wear. Seeing his puzzlement, the girl laughed and pulled the hat off. He looked down in amazement. Dark hair fell to her shoulders, her skin had the healthy bloom of outside work, black eyes danced up at him. A smile spread across his face.

'Colette?' he exclaimed, swinging himself down from his saddle and landing at her feet. 'How you have changed ...

where is the pale little mouse that I left behind me?'

'Probably still sitting under the mulberry tree – the one you were to wave at as you left!'

Gaston was instantly mortified. 'Oh, that was awful of me. I did remember, you know. I actually turned back, but by then it was too late!'

'Well it's not too late to beg forgiveness now.' Colette tried to look severe.

Going down on one knee on uneven ground was not a manoeuvre that Gaston had tried before. All went well until he gracefully lowered his seat on to the spur on his upturned heel. He shot to his feet with a yelp of pain, and naturally had to hold on to somebody.

'They never taught us to do that,' Gaston said laughing as he released Colette and dusted his knee. 'I am truly sorry though.'

'Ride on down. Maman has been waiting for you since dawn. I have just one more section to look at,' Colette said, suppressing her laughter.

As Gaston rode down the hill he was in high spirits; wait until he told the boys in the barracks about his mishap! And what a difference in Colette – happy, confident, flirtatious even! This could turn out to be a very interesting home leave. He would make a formal entry for Maman's sake, then he would cast his uniform aside, put on his civilian clothes again, and seek out Colette. He would flirt with her, and charm her and, if he was lucky, even snatch the occasional kiss. He felt like a seventeen-year-old, and resolved to behave like one. Plenty of time to be nineteen when he put on his uniform again.

And that was more or less how it turned out, even down to the stolen kisses. When the migrants arrived for the harvest Gaston found that Colette had taken his place from him. The workers remembered her from last year and she made sure that Gaston paid for the latest kiss by ordering him about until he told her that he would do nothing more until he'd had another.

The Count came during the harvest, sensibly dressed in common clothes, a modest cockade in his buttonhole. Rumours that he was now dressing as a *sans-culotte* seemed to have been exaggerated.

Late that night Colette and Gaston walked up through the shattered vines and sat close together, looking down onto the valley. Colette thought she had never been so happy.

All too soon it was over; Gaston's legs were still purple from treading the grapes when he pulled on his freshly laundered trousers and struggled into his tighter-fitting uniform. When he rode out below the mulberry tree he blew a flight of kisses to his dark eyed 'cousin,' and swore that he'd never touch another girl's lips until he rode home to her again. But it was 1793 and no one in France knew what the next day might bring.

⌒⦚∭⦚∼

Colette had never been invited up to M. Morteau's retreat above the fermentation rooms. No one, other than M. Brouchard the miller, went up uninvited; they would call up from below if they wanted attention. He must have seen Colette staring forlornly at the rain, which was falling like stair rods on the still purple cobbles of the yard.

'Come, Colette. I want to show you where this year's vintage came from.'

It was a relief to be occupied, after the emptiness that Gaston had left behind him. Colette climbed the steep loft steps and emerged into a bright attic. A long dormer window gave a sweeping view of the grey rain-soaked slopes; they were not going to see much from here today. But M. Morteau wasn't interested in the view; he had rolled back the oiled linen cover of a map that was spread on the table. Colette was amazed to see that every field, plot, and even row, of vines was in its correct place. She looked closely at the tiny writing and saw that the grape varieties were indicated, together with other details of the plots. She was flabbergasted. There was no mention of 'dunderheads', or even 'scholarship classes' here; this was the science behind his art, and he was explaining it to her! Colette concentrated until her mind could hold no more information. Eventually the lesson was over and M. Morteau rolled down the protective cloth.

'Have I tired you, my dear?'

'No ... no, but I have so much to learn.' And then a thought struck her: surely this was Gaston's place?

'Papa,' she said, using the endearment for the first time, 'why do you let Gaston go off to be a soldier, when you could have him here helping you?' There was a pause; had she gone too far, she wondered? But he was just thinking about his reply.

'Firstly, he wanted to go. Perhaps that is enough, but your question deserves a better answer. Come down, we will open a bottle for dinner and drink his health.' They descended past the vats, and down again to a special cellar beneath. Here the bottled wines were stored, the glass balloons tipped on their sides in sand so that their corks were always moist. It took Papa Morteau a moment or two to find the bottle he wanted. He drew the cork carefully and poured out half a glass for each of them. They spun the wine in the glass, looked at it against the light of a candle, and sniffed the bouquet; Colette was familiar with the routine by now. Papa watched while she tasted, and smiled when her eyebrows shot up. The first taste had been strong, even a little bitter – a shock to the palate – but now, as the wine rolled about her mouth, it lost its aggression and became warm and mellow as its strength developed. 'Does that remind you of anyone?'

'Gaston?' Colette hazarded. Papa Morteau laughed. 'When that wine was made it was undrinkable, and if it had been bottled like that it would have done the drinker an injury. But I gave it its head, let it work off its aggression, its energy, in good oak barrels. Not to everyone's taste, I'll admit.'

'Oh, I like it!' said Colette, and she blushed.

'Well, we'll bring it in now and have it, as all wine should be had, with some food.' As they walked over the gleaming cobbles Papa Morteau said something that Colette was to remember later.

'This energy, this aggression, it's in the family, you know, this latent energy. I just wish I'd had the bottling of his cousin, the Count.'

'He seemed very personable to me,' Colette said.

'Personable, yes, but reliable, no. I have made wines that bottle true, and others that are wayward: one bottle has all the qualities of a great vintage, while the next is undrinkable. Colette, my dear, do me a kindness and steer clear of cousin Auguste du Bois.'

No sooner had Gaston gone than the guillotine began its march through the provinces, and no one knew which way the gruesome cavalcade would turn. People at risk began to buy favours, knowing that it was the only way to ensure security in a time when the often secret votes of friends and neighbours could determine your fate. The Count du Bois found that portions of his vineyard made most acceptable gifts to the shopkeepers and tradesmen who might hold the cards against him if a vote for his life came up. The fact that these men knew nothing about making wine didn't matter; they could grandly refer to: 'My vineyards in Les Clos du Bois.'

For once in his life Paul Morteau dug in his heels; he would have nothing to do with these charlatans. They could tend their own vines, and make their own wine – or vinegar – if they chose. Nevertheless, Colette would often find him, close to tears, gazing out helplessly over the neglected slopes. She would take him by the arm then and steer him back on to the Count's diminishing acres and point out some fungus or ask about a pruning problem to distract his attention. She even suggested that he should write to Gaston about the problem, but M. Brouchard advised against it. If the censors came upon a letter complaining that the Count was giving land to deserving members of the Revolution, they might interpret this as treason.

CHAPTER 9

The Corsican General

Pierre and Marcel, having noticed that Lieutenant Morteau had not asked for Louise's portrait since they had entered Paris, made a formal request for the picture so that they could display it in their mess in the barracks. There was to be a regimental banquet and the cadets thought it would give them a certain status among the other cadets to show off the spoils of war. At first Louise was disconcerted at being the subject of so many eyes, but she soon realised that they had no holding power; they just passed over her like ripples breaking on a shore, not unpleasing, but not demanding either. From time to time, however, she would sense that someone had come along who was engaging with her.

'You, Cadet... you seem to be guarding this young lady. Do you know where she comes from?' There was the clatter of someone coming to attention. It was Pierre who answered, his voice as tight and rigid as the boy himself.

'From Holland, sir. She belongs to Lieutenant Morteau, *Monsieur le Général.*'

'Not stolen, I hope. The Dutch are our allies now.'

'Oh no, sir. He rescued her from a canal; another minute and she would have drow ... I mean it would have sunk, sir.'

'Here, Monsieur Durand!' the General called, 'You are the expert. Have a look at this.' Louise was aware of their examination; Monsieur Durand was leaning close.

'You know, the brushwork is quite exceptional. Look at the Turkey carpet, so much said with so few strokes. If only we had a signature. I would place it in style somewhere between Rembrandt and Vermeer, both masters at the very top. I'd give a king's ransom for it if it had a signature, or a thousand acres without.'

'I bet young Morteau has no idea how much it is worth. He's a good lad, and he has luck on his side ... did I tell you about crossing the Rhine?' The voices faded away, leaving Louise stunned at her worth, but delighted to hear Pieter's work on the carpet praised.

But Louise's worth meant little to the young cadets who paraded past her in their dress uniforms, as proud as bantam cocks. They had no shortage of damsels to satisfy their yearnings for female company and so they gave Louise only passing attention.

The banquet over, the regular routine of the regiment was re-established. The larger waves of sound and activity that swept the barracks also swept over Louise. Sudden orders would be shouted, there would be an immense hubbub, and then silence. The mess would empty and the barracks become bathed in that extra peace that only follows the exit of twenty or so boys.

Left alone, Louise began to think. She thought about Gaston and the intensity of their shared experience. She could almost feel the light movement of his hands on her hair. It was an illusion of course – a product of their imaginations working together – but what an illusion, what a gift. She remembered the Master's voice shouting, "Don't move", his hands held out, beseeching her to hold her pose. That's when it had begun, his gift of life, this immortality. Surely it was a gift for the good, but yet … perhaps Gaston had been right and she could be hurt. When young Pierre suddenly spoke to her, she was startled out of her wits. She hadn't noticed him standing in front of her, silently plucking up courage to speak.

Pierre had been sick. He had wandered about the barracks feeling more and more lonely, homesick and worried. He had come into the mess looking for food that he didn't really want and was about to drift out again when his eye met Louise's. He stopped in front of the portrait.

'I know you can't answer …' he whispered, 'but I must talk to someone.' He hesitated, and Louise could feel his mind pulling at her. Where had he got the idea of talking to her? She liked Pierre, but she was nervous. What had happened? First Gaston, and now Pierre. Had her immersion in the canal washed away some protective patina, or was it just that these young revolutionaries had the same energy that had charged the Master when he painted her? Perhaps she should resist him – shut her mind down – as she had learned to do sometimes with Gaston, but yet the boy seemed to be in trouble.

'Go on,' she willed him, and the lad's face cleared almost as if she had spoken.

'It's about Jeannine,' he said. 'I'm worried, I haven't seen her for almost a year … she doesn't write…' His lip began to tremble, and he bit on it so hard that Louise thought it might bleed.

Louise found that she could guide his thoughts, after a fashion. She listened patiently to his heart-torn yearnings for the miller's daughter on his father's small estate in Normandy. From his description she suspected that the girl had a roving eye. She tried to direct him to happier memories, and soon she was hearing about his home, about cattle knee deep in green grass, about orchards laden with apples, and about cider making. She heard about his friends and how he used to join the village boys who roamed the forests in groups, keeping in touch with each other by using high cat-calls that carried for miles and that no one else could under-stand. He was about to demonstrate when there was a crash at the door and Marcel burst in.

'Ho, Pierre. Worshipping our ladyship?' The older boy clattered over with the clumsy swagger of a cavalryman without his horse, and stood in front of Louise, appraising her shrewdly.

'I didn't think you were pretty at first, Mam'selle Louise, but by God just now you look good to me.' He looked at Pierre, who was blushing uncomfortably, laughed and punched him on his shoulder. 'Glad you're better... *Mon Dieu*, I could eat a horse.' He sniffed at the smell of roasting meat from the kitchens. 'Probably will too, that old saddle-sored hack from the baggage train, by the smell of him.' Pierre's face changed from pink to green as he allowed Marcel to lead him out.

The following day, Pierre, still on sick leave but visibly better, crept up on her again. 'Mademoiselle Louise?' he whispered, and she smiled to herself at the vision of a small boy slipping quietly through the mottled light of a Nor-mandy forest. What he said next however brought her back to the present with a jolt. 'Lieutenant Morteau is taking up service with the Sultan of Turkey!'

'What! ... Turkey?' she said aloud, though neither of them noticed.

'The day before I went sick he offered to come with me while I tried out a new horse that one of the senior cadets from the Hussars of Conflans wants to sell to repay a gambling debt. Lieutenant Morteau said we should give it a good gallop in the Bois du Boulogne to make sure it was sound. Unfortunately she went lame when we were far from home so, rather than returning late through the woods, we stayed the night in an inn on the other side of the forest. We had to share a room because the inn was full. We met an artillery officer in the taproom there who had seen action at Toulon. I was tired, and disappointed about the horse, who, it turned out, had a cracked hoof, which the Cadet who was selling her must have known. I left them talking and went to bed. I didn't hear Gaston ... I mean, the Lieutenant ... come to bed but I woke to hear him talking in his sleep. He was saying something about the *noyades* and seemed to be very ups–'

'What are these *noyades*, Pierre?' Louise interrupted; she had heard the word before.

'I don't know, a drowning accident perhaps. It was something that happened in Nantes. Raoul shut Marcel up when he asked him about them.' Louise nodded to herself; she remembered now.

'Go on.'

'Well, suddenly he shouted, "*Vive le Roi!*" at the top of his voice. I was terrified. The inn was crowded, and I was sure someone would hear; it's certain death to shout for the King! I shook him. He didn't wake, but he stopped talking. In the morning I told him what had happened. He said something very strange: "It's not a king I plan to join, Pierre, but a sultan: the Sultan of Turkey." Oh, Mademoiselle Louise, what will I do if he goes off to... to *Turkey?*'

'Would it worry you, Pierre?'

'Oh yes. I don't know what I'd do. When Lieutenant Morteau came and billeted on our estate last spring with his hussars, I wanted nothing but to become a hussar in his troop, and to wear his uniform and ride his beautiful horses. I thought him the most wonderful man in the whole world – I still do. When they had been with us for a week, my father told me that he was making arrangements for me to go as a cadet with Lieutenant Morteau. I was so proud. I was convinced that just putting on the uniform would make a man of me.' Pierre looked at the floor and shuffled his feet.

'All during our mission in Holland I was happy. But here in Paris I am under other commanders and I know now that I am no fighter, not like Marcel. I still love the men, and the horses, but there is something wrong with me; I feel sick even when I have to practice sticking my sabre into a sack of sawdust. On our way through Belgium, Lieutenant Morteau ordered me to pull a peasant out of a ditch. I've been teased about it, but I enjoyed it. I helped other people on the road too after that.' He smiled ruefully; 'You see, I'm really just a farmer at heart.'

'Can't you go home?' asked Louise.

'No. My father is under arrest. Our house is sealed and my mother and sisters are in lodgings. If I go to them I will just make things worse.'

'Then you must follow Gaston.'

'I don't think the Sultan of Turkey is looking for farmers.' Louise was at a loss for an answer to that.

'So, what happens next?'

'You remember the artillery officer we met in the inn that night? Well, he's given the lieutenant an introduction to an out-of-work general who's planning to take up arms with the Sultan of Turkey. He has an appointment to see him tonight. He wants me to go with him, and he has sworn me to secrecy.'

'What on earth is a French general doing going to Turkey?'

'I think he backed the wrong man in the Revolution. The Sultan is always looking for mercenaries, and he pays well. Now, I must go to the lieutenant's room. We will change there and then ride to that same inn beyond the Bois du Boulogne. I shouldn't have told you ...' The boy's lip began to tremble. 'But I had to talk to someone.'

Louise had a panicky feeling that Gaston was slipping away from her. Gaston, a mercenary! She must do everything in her power to stop him.

'Pierre, listen; take me to Gaston now. Tell him you are afraid the picture will be damaged in one of these fights you boys are so fond of having. Can you do that for me?'

'Of course, but I must be quick, or the other boys will be back.'

———✦———

'What have I forgotten, Pierre, this damned outfit seems all wrong?' Gaston, in civilian clothes, was tweaking at the cravat at his throat. He sniffed his sleeve, 'Go down to our landlady, Pierre, and get a clothes-brush for me. I think I have mildew.'

When Pierre had arrived, carrying Louise's picture, Gaston had seemed uninterested, waving it into a corner of the room. Louise sensed straight away that he was up to something and he was trying to keep her out of it. The door closed and Pierre's footsteps receded down the stairs.

'What you have forgotten is me,' said Louise, and had the satisfaction of seeing Gaston jump.

'You shouldn't do that sort of thing to me! What's this Pierre tells me about you stirring up trouble in the barracks?'

'Just boys fighting; it's something they do until they grow up and learn sense.' Gaston didn't notice the jibe, so she persisted. 'Where are you going?'

Gaston shrugged, 'To meet an out-of-work general I heard about ...'

'At an inn in the Bois de Boulogne?' Gaston's head jerked up in alarm.

'How do you know that?'

'Pierre told me.'

'*Sacrédieu!* You must not start appearing to Pierre. I forbid it!'

'I'm *not* appearing to him, but I can't stop him if he talks to me, and I'm not one of your soldiers that you can order around!' With an effort, Louise calmed herself; she mustn't betray Pierre, but she mustn't let Gaston lock her out of his mind.

'What did he say? Oh my God, this will be all over Paris. Have you heard of the guillotine? Heads have rolled for less!'

'Like shouting for the king in your sleep? You needn't worry – Pierre only talks to pictures. He said that you are going to take up service with the Sultan of Turkey?'

'Can't you understand ... this is confidential. Damn it, Louise, it is none of your business.'

'Don't swear at me, Gaston Morteau. You know perfectly well that if you are hiding it from me, you are hiding it from yourself.'

'Well, I am going anyway,' Gaston said defiantly, 'And you can't come; you're wearing that silly uniform, and we're in civilian dress.'

'If we had time you could think up a nice fashionable riding habit for me,' Louise said, trying to diffuse some of the tension. 'But what does it matter how I am dressed? It's only you who can see me.'

'I'll imagine you on a mule,' he said vindictively.

There were steps on the stairs.

'Shhh, Pierre's coming.' Gaston was still facing Louise when the door opened.

Pierre came in carrying a brush that looked to Louise like a yard broom. 'You look all right from behind, sir,' he said, and applied the brush vigorously to Gaston's back. Gaston made one last warning grimace towards Louise, and then held his breath against the swirl of dust. Louise had won that battle; she was tempted to do a cheeky pirouette, but she wasn't completely sure that Pierre would not see her.

Winter still held its grip on the Paris basin. It was dusk as they trotted down the sandy track that wound through the Bois du Boulogne, retracing Gaston and Pierre's journey of a few nights before. Their horses' breaths blew back in fragrant clouds. Louise kept to the rear; she had made her point and had no wish to make Gaston self-conscious through her presence. It was strange how civilian clothes changed their profiles. The sharp angles of the soldier's garb had been replaced by the shapelessness of hat and cloak. They had been talking about the footpads that frequented the forest, so she was reassured to see the tips of their swords protruding from beneath their cloaks; they would have pistols as well. The light was failing, and the trees seemed to be crowding in on them. She rode up a little closer.

The inn yard was noisy and full of jostling movement; Pierre stabled the two horses while Gaston haggled for a room. He had forgotten all about Louise now, her imagined horse needed no stabling, so she stayed out of sight. She had made her point; and she had the feeling that Gaston was not really sorry to have lost that battle.

'Come on, Louise, if I am to be on time we must go.' Pierre had been sent off to amuse himself. Gaston closed the cover of his watch with a snap. He glanced at the note of introduction. 'Général Napoleon Bonaparte,' he rehearsed, before throwing it into the fire. Louise thought Gaston looked very smart. He was wearing a cutaway coat over white trousers. His hair, released from its usual plaits, curled elegantly to the top of his shoulders. The plaits – a source of pride – were a characteristic of the Hussars, who could not afford to have loose hair blowing into their eyes. She followed him through a labyrinth of corridors to a part of the inn where the rooms were larger, small suites in fact. Here he checked his watch again, acknowledged her presence with a nod, and knocked.

'*Entrez.*' Louise slipped into the room behind Gaston and then moved quickly into the deepest shadow she could find. Despite her unease about this meeting, she was glad to be back doing things with him. Apart from her encounters with Pierre, life in the barracks had been dull.

Gaston felt nervous. He knew nothing of politics, but he had no doubts about the danger of consorting with a general who was about to abandon France for a foreign army. The general – if it was he – had his back to him and was staring into the fire. Gaston was disappointed at what he saw. The man was quite short, lank hair fell to the top of his shoulders, and he was wearing a dressing gown.

'Monsieur le Général Bonaparte,' Gaston said, bowing.

He had noticed a mirror over the fireplace; the man could see him.

'You are on time, Lieutenant Morteau,' the General said, without turning, 'but I expected no less. And how is your friend General Daendels? It must have been nice to support a friend of your family at his moment of triumph.'

'He is well, I believe,' Gaston replied, amazed. How in God's name did this obscure general know his family history? Bonaparte had a strong accent and Gaston vaguely remembered someone saying he was from one of the islands in the Mediterranean ... Corsica perhaps? He was still adjusting his thoughts when the General turned and stood with his back to the fire, looking him up and down as if he was on parade. Gaston realised with surprise that he was really quite young, in his late twenties? His eyes were grey, humourless perhaps, but curiously penetrating. For some reason it seemed important to Gaston to have their approval. The General smiled thinly and said:

'You cavalrymen never look your best in civilian clothes. It's the way you turn in your toes, afraid that you will lock your spurs together.' He laughed dryly. Gaston drew himself up, automatically responding to anything that might be an insult to the hussars. All he knew about this man was that he was a gunnery officer who had distinguished himself at the relief of Toulon, but gunners do not make fun of hussars! The General saw Gaston stiffen. 'I like a little pride, Morteau,' he said, 'but tell me, when you choose a horse, Lieutenant, do you not ask yourself if it has anything between its ears?' This really. *was* an insult; Gaston was furious – it was an old joke in the army that cavalry officers, for all their splendour, had fewer brains than their horses. He was about to turn on his heel and walk out when he caught sight of Louise in the shadows. She was grinning, but she was shaking her head. If he walked out in high dudgeon now, who would have won the point? He pulled himself together just in time.

'Indeed, General, the horse must be worthy of the man, but also – if I may say so – the man must be worthy of the horse.' *Touché*, he thought. But his examination was not over yet. For the next half hour he stood more or less to attention while the small general marched up and down the room in his dressing gown, his hands clasped firmly behind his back, and interrogated Gaston about his movements, his rapid promotion, and the success of the Dutch campaign. When Gaston told him how General Daendels had negotiated the peace with the Dutch, the general sighed.

'Would that all battles could be won without fighting. So it fell to your lot to bring the news to Paris?'

'No, General, it was Captain Sorel of the Staff who was the courier, I just provided the escort.'

'And it was you who decided that the ice would hold when you took him across the Rhine. Wasn't that a risk?'

'Yes, but it saved us days of travel. I was assured that speed was of the essence; I was just lucky.'

'Just lucky! Never underestimate luck, my boy, a good officer makes his own luck.' Then, without warning, he turned on Gaston with the lightning strike of a snake. 'If speed was of the essence, Lieutenant Morteau, what in the devil's name were you doing hauling a carriage across Europe; couldn't this Captain Sorel ride a horse?'

'They were my orders, General ... protocol apparently: "The status of the courier to be maintained."' Even as he spoke he felt a sudden chill invade the room.

'It was *folly*, Morteau, not just foolishness but *folly!*' The

General was staring up into Gaston's face. Gaston had never seen cold rage like it. The man was actually hissing at him. 'Here was information of the utmost importance to your country, mired in the roads to Mons. It took you weeks to get that man to Paris. How long would it have taken you without that damned carriage?' The general had hooked a finger through Gaston's buttonhole and was holding him fast.

'In as many days as it took weeks, General,' Gaston admitted. The little man nodded. He had made his point; his anger went as quickly as it had come.

'Listen to me,' the voice was suddenly soft, even affectionate. 'One day, Lieutenant Morteau, you will bring me news of a victory, one of yours perhaps. Promise me that your horse will die under you before you lose even an hour in getting me the news.' Then he chuckled, 'You may not have heard, but they tell me the ice broke up the day after your crossing; you did well.' He reached up and gave Gaston a tweak on the ear. 'Now Lieutenant, I think we can do business. I will tell you the details later and you can confirm your decision in a letter. For now let us relax, sit down and talk war; the sound of my guns may represent the beating heart of an army, but as you say, the cavalry are its eyes and ears.'

As the two men sat together, bent over a small map-strewn table, talking about reconnaissance, scouting, spies and intelligence, Louise could feel Gaston's mind receding from her. With a sinking heart, she knew that Gaston was now as much in this man's thrall as young Pierre had been in thrall to him. He would go to Turkey.

It was time for her to leave, but just as she was about to fade away the General asked Gaston a question that she had been longing to ask him herself.

'Lieutenant Morteau, you are doing well in the Hussars of Auxerre, so why leave France to come with me to Turkey?' There was a long pause. When Gaston replied his voice had a strange intensity, and Louise knew that he was speaking from his heart.

'General, I have witnessed Frenchmen fighting Frenchmen; I now know that I want no part in the destruction of my own people.' He paused, and Louise realised that their minds were still in tune, because she saw, through his mind, a stretch of grey water at dusk. A shadow lay low in the water, and there were strange cries in the distance. Then, quite close, she heard a girl's voice saying; "No, those are the *noyades* ... silly!" There it was – that word again – what did it mean?

The General was speaking. 'It angers me too. Here we are, killing our own people in their thousands, when those same lives could more profitably be expended to the glory of France.'

'At home or on foreign fields?' Gaston asked.

'Either. War is the only way to distract us from our present folly. Call back the Prussians, I say! At the moment your Frenchman is like the child of a cruel father, all he can do is hate and resent the tyranny of the father. To coerce the peasant we need to portray France not as his father but as his mother, his hearth, and his home, something to love, to protect, and to defend with his life. The Terror is a wasteful tool. Peasants don't march for liberty or equality or fraternity, but they will fight with passion for the things familiar to them. And what is more familiar to someone than his mother? Give me ten thousand peasants, trained in arms, fighting *chacun pour sa mère*, and nothing will stop us.' The

General rose to his feet and began pacing up and down. 'For all that I won back Toulouse for them, I am cast adrift. "Robespierre's man," they call me.' His voice was bitter; 'I'm nobody's man, Morteau, but my own! They have cut off Robespierre's head, and I don't propose to add to the waste by offering them mine. Come …' he said sitting down again, 'you say you are the eyes of the army, tell me how you will see that your intelligence gets back to me.'

Louise did not attempt to follow their discussion, but stood back, dazed by what she had heard. Tens of thousands of peasants to be expended for this little man's ambition! Yet there was something about him that was compelling, even if terrifying. She remembered a day long ago in her native Holland. Father had taken her out along the sea dykes when high tides and an on-shore wind had piled the ocean up against the barrier. The wind-whipped waves splashed at their feet. She had turned her face into the wind and shouted her defiance. But Father had swept his cloak about her and warned: 'Be careful what you say to the waves, my dear, just one small breach in the dyke and that ocean will sweep in and cover our land.' This General Bonaparte had eyes that were the same sea-grey as that ocean, and his energy had the same feeling of power as that frustrated sea. 'Go away little man,' she whispered. 'Go off to Turkey, and leave my Gaston behind.' Neither of them heard her appeal. She had lost Gaston's mind to a stronger one than hers, and she faded from the room.

CHAPTER 10

The Noyades

The following day Gaston was nervous but excited. He made several attempts to get Louise to appear but she resisted. She knew that he was still under the influence of his new friend Bonaparte, and recognised that he, for the moment, was the dominant force. She had to find a chink in Gaston's armour – and she thought she knew of one that might work – but she must choose her own moment. It was, however, Gaston who forced the pace.

Darkness had fallen. Gaston was bent over a small table. The only source of light was a candle that stood beside him. Louise could hear the dry sound of a quill rasping on paper. The light, reflecting off the paper, lit his face from below, and she was reminded of a painting of another letter-writer that had hung in the Master's studio in Delft all those years ago. She had liked it, but the Master had dismissed it as being in the manner of Caravaggio: *A trick done with mirrors*. She could feel Gaston's concentration flowing away from her like a stream.

'Gaston?' she said. 'Where are you going?'

He pursed his lips. 'I'm not *going* anywhere. I'm just writing a letter.'

Louise moved towards him. He put his quill down but laid it so that it covered what he had been writing.

'Am I disturbing you?' she asked.

'You always disturb me, Mademoiselle Eeden.' He seemed nervous.

'Who are you writing to?'

'I don't think that's any of your business!'

'Of course it's my business. You're writing to General Bonaparte, aren't you? You've decided to go to Turkey.'

'You can come too, you know. Well, why not? Don't you like the idea of a Turkish harem?' Gaston looked slyly up at her, his eyebrows arched. Louise was furious.

'Don't you speak to me, or look at me like that, Gaston Morteau! You may take a painted portrait to Turkey if you wish, but don't expect to find *me* there. I don't want to go anywhere with a man who has cut himself off from where his heart and soul lie. Go to Turkey and you will be abandoning the Gaston you might have been, just as you will be abandoning young Pierre. What's driving you away, Gaston … your nightmares?' He looked away. 'No, don't turn your back on me. There's no point; you won't be able to escape from your dreams, they'll follow you wherever you hide.' He turned towards her as if to say something, and she saw a flicker of uncertainty in his eyes. She thrust for home. 'I know about your nightmares, remember? I sat beside you during your fever, when you were dreaming about the *noyades*. Then, the other night in the inn you scared young Pierre with a shout of "*Vive le Roi.*" Tell me about the *noyades*, Gaston. Then, I promise, you can write your letter in peace.'

'Damn you, Louise,' he breathed. 'Damn you a thousand times.' But his head had dropped; he rested it on his hands. Then he made one last effort. 'Don't you see – I want to get *away* from all this; I want to go forward, not back.'

'But you are not going forward, you are running away.

Just tell me what happened in Nantes, then I will be quiet.'

He closed his eyes, and then said in a low voice: 'There was a girl involved. I feel ... a bit ashamed.'

'On account of me?'

'You ... and another.' Of course; she remembered a gnarled old tree above a country road, and a girl waiting. Louise felt a tiny stab of pain.

'Never mind,' she said, 'just tell it to me as it was.'

Gaston turned from the table and rested his hands on his knees as Louise sank down and sat cross-legged on the floor at his feet. He took a deep breath and, fixing his eyes on a point above Louise's head, he began: 'Last October, thirty thousand armed men from an area known as the Vendée, who were loyal to the King and to their priests, crossed the Loire, the great river that divides western France into north and south.'

'Loyal to priests?' Louise queried.

'Many priests refused to swear allegiance to the civil authorities, saying that they wouldn't take an oath to an atheist Republic. Between the Royalists and the priests they took ... oh ... hundreds of thousands of peasants – men like the ones you saw at the Pont de Chasse, armed with scythes, rusting swords and fowling pieces. These were the Vendéeans. Over the river they poured, crossing at bridges, in boats, and at fords ... they were like lemmings. Once across, they headed north. They had just one idea, and that was to get to the little port of Granville on the Normandy coast. Here they were told that they would find a fleet from England with an émigré army – the Royalists who had fled the Revolution – and together they would march on Paris and the monarchy would be restored. It was all a cruel lie. They fought, by God they fought; they captured cities, laid waste ... but when they got to the coast, the port was sealed and there was not a sail in sight. Winter was approaching; they had eaten everything edible in a swathe across France and now they had to return down the same route, exhausted, harried, and starving. When at last they reached the Loire again they found the bridges blocked, the fords held against them, and their boats burned. It was then that the real slaughter began.

'All that autumn in Auxerre we heard of the progress of the Vendéeans, and were frustrated to be out of the action, now it seemed that it was all over. Then, just before Christmas last year we got our call.' Gaston paused, and then he shook his head and went on. 'A politico, a member of the government from Paris, needed an escort to Nantes. We all applied to be let go.' He gave a wry smile, 'I must have clamoured loudest. I was a different man then, Louise. I was intense, proud ... full of zeal to prove myself and my troop. The Republic was a glorious ideal. When the guillotine dropped in the name of the Republic I washed away my revulsion, with the same ease that the servants of the Republic wash away the blood from under the guillotine today. I was pure, I was brave, and what – in my imagination – I did, I did for France ...' He flipped a hand and sighed.

'We took the road south and west until we met the Loire and then followed the river towards its mouth. To begin with we were relaxed. Our politico needed to inspect several of the great chateaux that lie along the Loire, to check that the seals put on them to prevent their owners returning were intact. In that way I trailed my spurs through the dust-sheeted rooms of some of the greatest chateaux of France.

'The signs of war increased as we moved west. The Vendéeans had burned whole villages for resisting them; so our forces had burned other villages for co-operating with them. I cannot describe the horrors we met. We passed columns of prisoners being marched till they died because their captors had run out of the lead to shoot them. I looked down into the despairing faces of my own countrymen: simple, uncomprehending peasants like the migrant workers that sing while they pick our vines and tread our grapes. But I told myself that their suffering was merited because of the terrible things they had done.

'When we got to Nantes even the semblance of order in the town was a relief. It's a port, situated on a wide shallow estuary. There were no more corpses beside the roads here. The soldiers wore real uniforms, not rags, and civilians no longer felt they had to dress like *sans-culottes*.'

'*Sans* ...?' Louise queried. Gaston explained about the Jacobin uniform.

'I went in search of a billet, and found space down by the docks. Here my men cleaned up and then set off into the town. It's extraordinary what the uniform of a hussar will do in a town full of infantry. We were hardly there an hour before I got an invitation to attend a dinner and reception put on by the harbour authority.

'There seemed to be no shortages here, not at any rate for officials of the Republic. Perhaps supplies came in by sea? I was put sitting beside a remarkably pretty girl who told me that her father was the port's doctor. We talked about hussars, which pleased me immensely, and she told me of the slaves from Africa that her father had to certify as fit for transportation to our colonies in the West Indies; Nantes, you see, is a slave port. After dinner, the reception room was hot, and the wine of Bordeaux, though light on the palate, is strong in the head. I suggested that she take my cloak and that we walk beside the water. She took my arm, I held her close against the cold, and felt her body soft against mine.'

Louise glanced up but Gaston's eyes were focused on the past.

'The noise of the city died away behind us. There was a full moon and a full tide. I had never seen the sea before. I was just telling her how strange and exciting it was for me to think that I could board a ship here in Nantes and sail to any port in the world, when a strange crying sound was carried to us from out in the water. I asked her if this could be the sound of whales. She laughed.

"'No, silly, those are the noyades. I thought a soldier would know that! Those are cries from the slave barges. The army has commandeered them for the Vendée prisoners; it was Papa's idea."

"Where do they take them? To the prison hulks?" I asked.

"'Oh no, that's not necessary. They load the boats quietly, after dark, until they are quite full, and take them out into the estuary. Then they sink them so that the prisoners drown. That's why they are called the noyades – the drownings. Papa says it's quite quick really. When the tide goes out they recover the hulks and start all over again."'

'We stood side by side, and I imagined the water rising … rising.' Gaston's voice tightened. 'Now that I knew what was happening, I understood that those were human voices I was hearing – voices raised in terror. The cries grew fainter and fainter. Then in the last silence a single voice rose clear over the water: "*Vive le Roi!*"

"*Les malheureux!*" I said, "poor souls."

'My pretty friend pressed my arm and called me an old softie … Forgive me, Louise, but as we walked, the musky scent she wore turned for me into the stink of death and the soft breast against my arm turned leprous in my mind. I saw the girl home, declined her invitation for a night-cap, and rushed headlong to the nearest tree, where I sicked up my heart.'

Louise remembered Raoul's voice: 'You'll feel better after that.' Raoul knew.

Gaston shook his head as if to clear away the memories of the past. He looked up at Louise, his face still haunted. 'It was then, kneeling beside that tree, that the prisoners we had passed on the road came alive in my mind as real people who had mothers and wives. I raged at the fanatics who had led them and I squirmed with shame at our own authority's mindless slaughter of the poor people. I learned later that two thousand people were drowned in the *noyades* alone. Louise, these were Frenchmen, the very people I had sworn to defend! The soldier in me died by that tree.'

'And what took its place?' Louise asked.

Gaston sighed sadly. 'The clown that you know – the parody of the chivalrous knight.'

'I would not be here if it were not for that chivalry,' Louise reminded him gently. 'So, what now?' she asked.

'I have vowed never again to take up arms against my countrymen. You were there with me when I met Bona-parte; I have found someone else who is dissatisfied with his lot, a general without a command. So he plans to go into the service of the Sultan of Turkey and he needs a few specialist young officers, like me, to go with him. This is my letter of acceptance.' Gaston made to pick up his pen again.

'But, Gaston, won't this be just the same as what you are trying to escape? More senseless slaughter, just in a different land?'

'At least they won't be French.'

'But they'll still be people! Gaston, you can't lose your humanity once you have found it. Don't you see you will find human beings wherever you raise your sword now? The damage has been done. I can almost forgive that wretched girl in Nantes because she has made a human being out of you. Why do you have to be a soldier? Can't you find yourself an army that doesn't fight!' She watched him sadly as he turned his back on her. He picked up his quill and held it over his inkpot, then with a sigh he put the pen down. He took the sheet of paper and held a corner over the candle flame. An orange ribbon of fire crept upward over the page. For a moment it underlined the salutation: *Monsieur le Général Bonaparte*, then it was gone. Gaston carried the ashes to the grate and turned to Louise with a look that dispelled any feeling of triumph she might have felt.

'You are interfering again, Mademoiselle Eeden. That could be my career in ashes in the grate.' He returned to his table and reached for a new sheet of paper.

'What are you going to do, Gaston?' She was anxious.

'Do I have to answer all your questions?' He sighed and his expression softened. 'Louise, I am going to do what I should have done long ago; open negotiations with the Count du Bois to buy some land so that I will have something to return to if I have to. As it stands now, if the Count got into trouble with the authorities, our livelihood would be in jeopardy. But on one matter I am firm; I will not remain in the army if it requires me to murder my own countrymen.' Louise wanted to ask about the Count, and about Gaston's family, but decided that this wasn't the moment.

Gaston had just finished the page and shook fine sand on it to dry the ink, when there was a sharp rap on the door.

'*Merde!*' he said as he turned the paper upside down on the desk. It was Marcel, the duty officer that night, looking excited. He saluted smartly and handed Gaston a blue envelope.

'Orders,' he said. Gaston broke the seal and examined the paper, holding it sideways in the light from the corridor.

'Good news, cadet. We leave for Auxerre tomorrow. We're going home. I will inspect the men at eight. For once you shouldn't have any trouble in getting them up.'

CHAPTER 11

Family Affairs

Louise could see that Gaston's mind was already preoccupied with the practicalities of an early departure. It was a point of honour with him to have as many as possible of his troop ready for the road within hours. There would always be men sick, horses lamed, baggage not ready, but the core of his troop must be there – the men immaculate, the horses groomed. She enjoyed these occasions and Gaston seemed to like having her around; he would talk to her, explaining, and not expecting any answers, but his energy would flow out to her and she would find her mind clear and lucid.

She had had time to shake off the near hypnotic effects of that interview with General Bonaparte. She was still shocked at the way both men had behaved, like schoolboys planning some fantastical adventure, talking of war and fighting and death as if the people who were to do the fighting were an expendable commodity. Death in war was no longer remote, it was immediate, and its threat made her realise how much Gaston meant to her. She did not share his faith in his own ability to survive in war. The thought of him lying dead or injured on some foreign battlefield was unbearable. Why was he a soldier? Did home mean so little to him that he would leave France and sell his sword to anyone who would give him a horse to ride? Louise could understand the excitement of being on campaign, and she could admire the magnificent uniforms, and wonder at the strange codes of honour that had them strutting about like fighting cocks. But Gaston was no fool. Was there really nothing to draw him back from this present insanity? The posting to Auxerre was only a reprieve. If there was only something – someone – to force Gaston to choose.

And maybe there was ... Louise remembered how she had shared Gaston's thoughts in the emotion-filled moments after he had told her about the engagement at the Pont de Chasse. In his mind she had seen a country road and a girl sitting beneath a gnarled old tree. Could this girl be someone to draw Gaston back to his home and his responsibilities there? Someone who could be an ally for her, Louise? She must make Gaston take her portrait with him when he went home on leave. Perhaps she could seek out this girl and they could work together to wean Gaston away from war.

For a moment Louise was filled with enthusiasm. She had never had a sister and had longed for a girl with whom she could share ... oh, so many things. But not ... not what? Gradually a new realisation crept through her, that there *was* something that she didn't want to share; she didn't want to *share* Gaston, she wanted him for her own.

The next day they departed for Auxerre in good order. The men were looking forward to home leave, and Louise was content for the moment not to dwell too much on the future. It was enough that Gaston was happy and encouraged her to ride with him. She allowed herself to be distracted as day by day their ride took them south up the Seine, and then branched up the Yonne towards Auxerre. As they rode up the precipitous road to the castle, their horses slipped and clattered on the cobbles and the city folk cheered and clapped the returning men of their own regiment of hussars.

Almost as soon as they arrived, those men whose homes were in the town began to depart on leave. Gaston was preoccupied with his report to his colonel. The cadets got disgracefully drunk, and had to be disciplined and set to mucking out the stables. Eventually the colonel slapped Gaston on the back, said he had done a good job, and told him to go on home.

'Why don't you take your two cadets,' he suggested, 'before they wreck the town. They don't have any family here, do they? You could put them to work in the vineyards.'

As if to make up for its recent harshness, winter had given way to an early spring. Gaston, together with a small troop of eight men and two cadets, none of them natives of the area, was on the road again, heading still further up the Yonne, towards Les Clos du Bois. The air was full of birdsong and the first crickets were trying out their bows. They stopped for lunch by a meadow, where the men were soon stretched out, half-dressed, in the sun. Gaston took a bottle of wine, some bread fresh from a village bakery downstream, and a slab of cheese, and climbed up to a spot under a tree from where he could keep an eye on everything but be private at the same time. Below him the river curved in a wide meander, spreading a sheet of gravel about it like a dancer's skirt. There the horses stood hock deep, dipping and raising their heads while they drank.

He would soon be home and he thought back to his homecoming of a year and a half ago. He smiled, remembering Colette and the flirtation they had enjoyed. He could still see her, laughing up at him as on the day he had arrived. He broke open his loaf and set about his meal with enthusiasm.

'I'd forgotten what it was like to feel hungry,' said Louise. Gaston put down his knife and his cheese with a sigh of mock exasperation.

'I climb all the way up here, just to be on my own, and who appears to disturb my peace but Mademoiselle Eeden. Do you want some?'

'Thank you, but I'll have to content myself with the idea.'

'Allow me to spread my cloak then!'

'Gaston, I like you, you get more like Don Quixote every day,' she laughed and sat down where the thin shade from the new leaves dappled the ground. 'How far have we to go now?'

'Not far, Louise, we're almost there. I am longing to see my family again, my mother and father, and–' he broke off. 'Also, as you know, I need to see my cousin, the Count du Bois. I am going to have to be nice to him, he holds my destiny in his hands.'

'What about General Bonaparte? Will he go to Turkey?'

'If he gets a command here in France, I think he will stay.'

'Would you join him … in France, if he asked you?'

'I might not have much choice, but just now I want to get home. You have made me think that I should keep my options open.'

'Tell me about your home, I know nothing about it or your family, or indeed the Count who seems to be so important in your lives. I'd like to hear, I really would.'

'May I speak between mouthfuls?' Louise settled herself and Gaston began. 'For more generations than we can remember, my family have been winemakers to the Count du Bois. Like I told you, it's not just a business arrangement because there are blood ties too, some of them even legitimate. My mother is a cousin of the Count.'

There was something romantic to Louise about the idea of a Count, so she asked: 'The Count. What's he like?'

'Charming, courtly... well that's the side he shows the world ...'

'Yes?' Louise queried.

'Oh, nothing ... just rumours ... but let me say that I'm glad he won't be able to see you; he has a reputation.'

'But I'll be able to see him!' Louise laughed. 'So, you are aristocracy?'

'No, but close enough to be uncomfortable. It is we who see to the tending of the chateau's vineyards: harvesting the grapes, and making the wine – some of the best in France, or so we claim. We supply the chateau, but we make our money on the rest of the wine we sell. The Count owns the land, even the house we live in. Up until now this was the perfect arrangement. Even though my mother's marriage contract gave us the right to buy our house, and a division of the vineyard if we wish, there was no pressing reason to change the existing situation. We had security, and my father had no wish to be a landowner. Where wine is concerned he is an artist, you see.'

'An artist like the Master who painted me?'

'No Louise, my father uses a different sort of palette, the palate of his mouth.' Gaston chuckled. 'For him his wines are living things. Now, with the Revolution, our security and our livelihood are threatened. The Count is a loose cannon, and I am afraid he might do something foolish. If he was forced to flee the country or lost his head on the guillotine, we would have nothing. I have written to the Count saying that I will be advising my parents to take up my mother's option and buy the land. If he has prepared the terms then it should be possible for us to come to an agreement while I am at home. I expect there will be a letter waiting for me.'

'Tell me about your father, he sounds interesting.'

'You will like him. Winemaking is his life and love. His vines and barrels are like his children; he talks to them. He says that each barrel is a child with some special talent to be tamed or nurtured and that he, like a teacher, has just a few years to find what that talent is, and bring it out into the open.' Louise smiled at the warmth in Gaston's voice; it was as if he was already picking up the comforting vibrations from his home soil.

'And you, are you an artist too?'

'Oh no, I am just a pupil. I can spot talent all right, but it will be years before I can make a good wine great. I was too impatient to apply myself as I should have. I wanted to see the world.' He laughed ruefully. 'Like poor Pierre I fell in love with the uniform. And also it seemed that the moment had arrived when we were about to make the New France, a more noble calling than making new wine, I thought. And now my first fermentation seems to have turned to vinegar.' Gaston picked up a twig and began to peel the bark off it with his nail. Could he really be thinking about coming home for good? Louise wondered. Gaston looked up at her with a disarming smile.

'Remember you told me to find myself an army that doesn't fight! Well, I started thinking about that, and I realised that there *is* another army – the army that descends on our valley each year. They sweep in from the village, both regular workers and casuals, women too; everyone has a task. Then come the migrant workers, as wild as Tartars and as difficult to manage. For the duration of the grape harvest they swarm, and they carry; they tip tall baskets of purple grapes into the presses, they sing, and then they tread the grapes. They get drunk and bloody each other's noses; the occasional knife is drawn, but that's all. There is your army, Louise, my army, and my heritage. We have the money to make the purchase, but we must secure the land *now*. It would be folly to resign my commission – if I could – and then find that I had nothing to return to.'

'You really mean it: you could leave the army?' asked Louise.

'It will be difficult, but surely the fighting will stop; then I might return. The vineyards are extensive and Father has no one to help with the management. You have made me dream again, Louise. Perhaps I will bring Pierre with me and show him that grapes are superior to apples.' Gaston chuckled. 'Come, let me take you to where the vines line the slopes like regiments ready for battle, and where my ancestors have crushed grapes since the Romans taught them how. Then you'll see the grapes coming in, each bloomed like a plum, and listen to the songs of the workers as they tread them to pulp. And there is someone there I would like you to meet.'

He stood up and brushed the crumbs off his knees. 'Look …' he said. 'The cadets are getting the men ready. Come on, we will be there in a couple of hours.'

They both rose in their stirrups as they topped the rise and looked down into the vineyards below, nestling in a semicircular valley scooped in the valley side. Louise gasped at the beauty of this tiny contained landscape. Here, laid out in a variety of geometric sections, were fields of ordered vines, each field with its own direction of planting as if drawn with a comb on the brown soil. The neatness and order spoke to her Dutch heart. The sweep of the vineyards drew her eye down to the terracotta roofs and the slender spire of the village church below. She heard Gaston murmur 'home!' and she smiled across at him. She looked for the chateau, but Gaston said that, true to its name, the Chateau du Bois, formerly a hunting lodge, was situated in the forest some miles away. He pointed to the blue haze of trees in the distance, but she couldn't see any sign of a building. There was something fascinating, mysterious even, about the idea of a chateau, hiding there in the heart of the forest. She hoped she would get to see it.

'Come on,' he said, 'I know a short cut.' With that he wheeled right, plunging down a path between the vines. As they rode, he explained over his shoulder how each plot varied according to its altitude and how it caught the sun. Louise had questions about the stony soil and the trellises on which the vines were trained, but Gaston had stopped answering her; something was troubling him. Suddenly he pulled up in a fury. 'My God, Louise, look at them. Look at the state of these vines. Something dreadful has happened. Is Father sick?'

Louise could only look at him in puzzlement; to her these vines appeared particularly healthy and lush. 'Look, woman,' he said impatiently, 'that's second year growth; these vines have not been pruned! *Mon Dieu*, is it all like this?' Now he was urging his horse on down, slipping on the gravelly soil. Louise looked ahead to where even worse disaster seemed to have struck, with the vines having been cut to the ground, but Gaston turned, relieved. 'Thank God, at least a part of the vineyard has been saved.' She gazed in wonder at the close-cropped stubs while Gaston absently pointed out the green shoots bursting from knobbly bases. 'This is how they should look. This is the home vineyard, so, whatever else, Father was alive at pruning time... I know his work. Excuse me Louise, I must go.' Without further explanation he spurred his mare down the slope, leaving Louise in a scatter of fine stones.

Louise did her utmost to keep up, feeling that Gaston was still holding her in his mind, as if in this moment of crisis he needed her support. Eventually she arrived in a wide cobbled yard where lean-to sheds housed unfamiliar agricultural instruments. An ancient labourer, his face as dark and as wizened as a walnut, was leading Gaston's horse away. Through open doors she glimpsed dark interiors with huge vats and barrels, and something that might be a winepress. There was a feeling of suspended activity. The whole yard had the air of a place that should be full of men, and of comings and goings.

A door into the house stood open. Louise could hear voices within. A short passage opened out into a vast kitchen, divided by a table that Louise was sure could seat twenty men. The voices came from a small group of people clustered near the fireplace where copper pots gleamed and flickered in the firelight. Gaston, his back to her, had his arms around a tall, distinguished-looking woman, his mother surely. And the man in stockinged feet who was watching them fondly must be his father. A girl stood in the shadows, observing the reunion. A kitchen wench perhaps? No, Louise decided, this girl was here of right. The girl waited until Gaston had greeted both his parents and then stepped forward.

'Welcome home, Gaston,' she said. Gaston turned and saw her for the first time. Louise could feel his thrill of recognition, like the electric crackle you get when you run your hand over silk. Where had she seen that profile before? It looked as if Gaston was going to give her a hug, but then he changed his mind.

'*Mademoiselle Colette*,' he said with a little bow.

'Well, don't I get a kiss too?' she asked, holding up a cheek. 'And why didn't you answer any of my letters?' she queried when he had bent and kissed her.

'Oh, but I have received none,' he said defensively. 'We were never in one place long enough for them to find us.'

'And your right hand ... has it been cut off?' Gaston looked at his hand. Then he blushed brick red. 'Or did you just forget, like the day you forgot to wave to me under the mulberry tree?'

'I ... I did write...'

'Twice.'

'Yes, just twice,' he said lamely. Louise was watching, trying hard not to feel jealous, envious of this girl's easy familiarity. 'Are you still helping Papa in the vineyards?' Gaston asked. The girl was smiling now; she had had her say. It was Madame Morteau who said acidly:

'And ruining her complexion in the process. If her poor mother ...'

'Now, now, my dear,' said her husband. 'We've been into all that.' The girl ... Colette... came up to Gaston, and took his hands briefly. An apology, perhaps, for her attack about his letters. Then she dropped her head, and in that movement Louise recognised the girl that Gaston had shown her, sitting under a gnarled old tree. So, that was what had happened: he had forgotten to wave and felt guilty about it.

146

The full extent of the disaster in the vineyards only emerged after hours of discussion. Gaston and his father talked and argued while his mother supervised the cooking and the household chores, joining them from time to time to correct something that had been said. Colette was included, but was mostly silent. Pierre came in with Louise's portrait. He put it up at one end of the kitchen, where the light was poor, but it was out of the way. No one paid any attention to it, except Colette, who wandered over and looked at it for a while. Papers were brought out and parchments flattened with work-hardened hands. Spectacles were taken on and off, gold coins were produced, counted, and declared too few. Colette offered her few jewels, but Madame refused to even contemplate such a breach of trust with Colette's 'poor mother'. And all the time, one single letter, whiter than the rest, lay conspicuously in the middle of the table.

Darkness fell. All but Gaston had retired to bed. He sat slumped at the end of the table. Louise emerged and sat in silence. Then, in a low voice, she said:

'What's happened, Gaston?'

'It's the Count, damn him … Remember I told you how he owns our vineyards? When the Revolution took place, rather than fleeing the country like most of the aristocracy, he decided to stay and embrace the people's cause. I respected him when he appeared sensibly dressed, with just a cockade in his buttonhole, at the grape harvest, but now it seems that he has been selling us out, just to save his skin. I never thought that the Terror, which was just beginning, might be a danger to us, but apparently the Count did, and has been working very hard to keep his head at any price.

'Well, the Count has kept his head, but it's we who've paid the price. Since I left he has been busying himself among the shopkeepers and lawyers and doctors and blacksmiths that make up the region's commune, and they now accept him as one of their own. Apparently one of his ways of showing solidarity with the cause has been to "donate" the wine that gave us our income to the "citizens" of the Revolutionary Council of the region. No sales means no income for us. Now the vineyards have begun to disappear, acre by acre, finding their way into the hands of these influential bourgeois – the people who might otherwise demand our dear cousin's head at the guillotine. As a reward for his citizenship, he has now been appointed the caretaker of his own chateau. *Plus ça change* ... nothing changes, does it?'

'What about your mother's entitlement?' Louise asked. 'You said that there'd be a letter waiting for you here.'

'Yes, there it is,' he indicated the envelope on the table. 'After half a page of compliments and salutations and expressions of his great love and esteem, he *regrets* however that, since the time of Mother's settlement, the price of the land has doubled.'

'Has it?'

'Not at all. I think he doubled it to make his gifts seem bigger. But if he lets us have it at its real value, the very people he wants to impress will say he has cheated them.'

'Well then, pay the price, whatever it is, otherwise you are slaves!' Louise felt her hopes slipping away. She could grow to love this old farmhouse, she liked the look of Colette, and she wanted them all to be happy here together. Above all, she wanted Gaston to be out of the army and away from war.

'It's no use, Louise,' Gaston waved wearily at the strewn

table. 'We've been through our books and checked everything. You see, as tenants we own nothing, and our savings
are running out. Father is not good at accounts. The long
and the short of it is that the Count sees our house and acres
as a last desperate card for him to play. If, by some change
in fortune, he finds himself facing the guillotine, the whole
house of cards will collapse, and we are at the bottom of the
pack. The winery will be finished because the new owners
all think that they can make wine themselves.

'I will ride out tomorrow and tell him that we refuse to
pay. I'll give him a piece of my mind too while I am at it.
Now for bed. All this discussion has exhausted me.'

Gaston did visit the Count, but he refused to tell Louise
anything about it. She guessed that he had scorned the
Count's demands, and had given him an earful at the same
time. Later that day the papers were cleared away and the
family took their places around the end of the huge table for
the serious matter of a late dinner. Louise had noticed how,
even yesterday at the height of the crisis, all discussion was
suspended when food was brought to the table, and
conversation subsided to a murmur as they addressed their
meals. The fare was simple but ample: soup, bread, a
steaming stew, and wine poured from a jug – sipped, rolled
in the mouth, and then swallowed – often with a low word
of comment or appreciation.

Two weeks passed and the household fell into what
Louise imagined was its regular routine. Gaston spent time
out in the vineyards with his father and with Colette, who
seemed to have a role in the winery. But all was not well.
Though Louise was not invited on his daily round, Gaston

had not forgotten her. In the evening he would sit hunched and tense at the table, nursing one glass of wine too many, until Louise would relent and take her place opposite to him. Eventually she decided to address the topic that had been on her mind.

'Tell me about Colette, Gaston,' she said. He reached to top up his glass, but put the bottle down again.

'She's an orphan, you know ...' he began, and then told Louise about the girl's background and how they had taken her into their family. 'When I left to join the hussars she was a pale little creature hardly looking her fourteen years. A year later, when I got home on leave she had changed into the beauty you see today.' Gaston was staring into the distance. Then he smiled, 'I was bowled over, Louise, intoxicated, we both were. For the whole month of the grape harvest we snatched every moment we could get together. It was an enchantment. But when I set out after the holiday, I would soon be a sub-lieutenant on active service, so I put her from my mind.'

But not completely, thought Louise.

'Then, two weeks ago, you and I rode in together. I was seriously considering buying myself out of the army, to help at home. I had come to hate civil war and it seemed a nice idea to settle down here with my family, including my pretty little 'cousin' Colette. What I did not expect was that I would walk into this kitchen and that Colette would walk out of the shadows and I would know then, and with absolute certainty, that this was the woman that I wanted to be my wife.'

Louise hoped her face did not betray her pain. She hadn't wanted even to *share* Gaston, now it seemed as though she would have no part in his love. How could she bear to be a bystander to his happiness?

Gaston sat silently, then he stood up and started walking about the kitchen. 'And then came the second surprise ... that letter ... the Count, my real cousin, dashing the cup from my grasp as I was lifting it my lips.' His voice rose bitterly. 'Damn the Count, damn and blast him forever. Father says that we are all part of the one vine, with the roots in the chateau and the fruit out here in the sun. Maybe... but that vine is coiling itself about our necks, it is strangling us, Louise. We must cut it through!' Gaston slashed down with an imaginary sabre as he spoke.

'I can't tie Colette to me with no prospect that I can support her, and soldiers aren't exactly bankable commodities.' He sat down again, his shoulders slumped. 'I have orders to return by the end of the week ... the usual spy scares. It will be you and me again, Louise, we must take to the road and make what we can of life.' Then, abruptly, he changed the subject. 'Oh, by the way, the boys have asked if they can have your portrait to show to the men in the bunkhouse. Most of them have joined us since the Dutch campaign. Is that all right?'

It wasn't all right. Louise felt battered and emotionally bruised. One minute her place was being usurped by Colette, the next she had Gaston to herself again; she didn't know what to feel. And now she was to be 'loaned out' for the men's entertainment. She didn't like the way Marcel looked at her, but she couldn't really object; the cadets had guarded her faithfully all the way from Holland, so perhaps they had a right to show her off if they wanted to. And just now she needed to get away from Gaston to think.

The plates remained to be cleared from the kitchen table, but

Colette was staring at Gaston, watching and thinking. He had explained his orders and how he would have to leave in the next two days. *You really want to go, don't you?* she thought. *You and your boys, and your picture.* She knew that something profound had happened between him and her, something far deeper than the carefree love that had burst over them at the time of the grape harvest, but now she could feel him withdrawing. Surely the problem with the Count could be sorted out, and didn't he know she would wait ... wait for him forever? Was he against her working in the fields with Papa? She noticed how he kept looking over to where the picture had stood. She wanted him to look at her. Suddenly her reverie was broken by the sounds of a sharp altercation outside. Footsteps were pounding down the passage towards them. The corporal burst in, saluted Gaston hurriedly, bent to his ear and gasped in a low voice.

'Excuse me, sir, but young Colbert and Beauchamp are setting up for a duel, sir.'

'Good God, the fools!' Gaston was out of the door, sending his chair clattering on its back, before the corporal had time to move.

It was late by the time the boys had been silenced, sentenced, and bound to keep the peace. The family, including Colette, had gone to bed; Gaston sat alone, his head in hands. Louise's portrait stood again at the end of the kitchen, slightly askew. She came over and sat beside him. He shook his head and said, half to himself:

'Young Pierre, of all people, drawing on Marcel and challenging him to a duel! You heard him do it?'

'Yes, Marcel was making suggestions about me; it wasn't

the first time. Pierre picked up something, a glove I think it was, and slapped Marcel in the face. That's when they started shouting.'

'Pierre was defending your honour? But Pierre's no fighter, he'll always hold back on the telling stroke. Not so Marcel, he'll deliver his stroke, even against a friend. I sometimes wish I'd never recruited Pierre; did I tell you that his family have all died in the Terror? I can't send him back to Normandy even if I wished to.'

'Gaston,' Louise said contritely. 'It's my fault, I should never have allowed Pierre to talk to me.'

'We'll leave tomorrow. Once we are on the move again the boys will be all right.'

But Louise had reached her decision. 'Gaston, I'm not coming with you. No, let me finish … I'm just a source of tension among the boys. Also, I like it here. Leave my picture behind, and I'll be waiting when you come back. I feel now as though my place is here. Leave the army, Gaston, as soon as you can, and then come back here; bring Pierre with you, and make something useful of your life.'

'You know that's what I want, Louise, but at the moment it looks as if my army pay will be needed here more than my labour in the vineyard. But it will very strange not to have you by my side.'

The small troop left the following morning, with both Pierre and Marcel reduced to the ranks. If they noticed that Louise's portrait had been left behind, neither of them dared mention it to their Lieutenant.

CHAPTER 12

A Meeting of Minds

Over her long years of solitude Louise had found that children, in particular, would stare at her portrait with a curious intensity. That was how Colette's stare felt; it pulled at Louise. She could feel the girl searching for her, wondering what was the meaning of this picture that Gaston had brought home. Madame Morteau was for hanging it in the parlour, out of the way, but Colette had persuaded her to leave it where it was for the moment. It was a connection with Gaston, though she wasn't sure if she was quite comfortable with it. The green of the girl's silk dress glowed in the permanent dusk of the kitchen, and the light that had slanted through the windows of the Master's studio in Delft a hundred and forty years before seemed to brighten that corner of the room. When taking a break from her work in the house, or after coming in from time spent with M. Morteau among the vats and barrels, Colette would stop and gaze for a few minutes at the portrait. Sometimes it was just to explore the quiet restfulness of the Dutch interior, but at other times her eyes would be drawn to the face of the girl in the portrait. Louise could feel the chemistry beginning to work between them; the girl's curiosity about her was mounting, and this in turn was creating the energy that Louise needed to make contact with her.

And one day Colette spoke to her. 'Who are you, then?

And why do you *look* at me like that?' It was sharp, and Louise was hurt; all she had been doing was trying to reach out to the girl. Colette moved away, and now her back was turned, and the moment was lost. Why had the Master painted her to look so demanding, Louise lamented? But as she did so another thought crept into her mind. Had she, in her heart of hearts, been as welcoming to Colette in her thoughts as she might have been? Was she jealous of her? It would have been nice – she had to admit – to have found that the girl she had seen in Gaston's mind was just a little bit of fluff, or better still, one like that spirited little chamber-maid in Brussels who had fended him off with a warming pan. Someone for Gaston to play with while he found more worthy companionship in Louise. She smiled ruefully.

She reckoned that Colette must be a little older than she, seventeen perhaps. In terms of colouring they were oppo-sites. While Louise was fair, Colette's dark brown hair fell to her shoulders. Her deep-set eyes were black and her skin, though not burned, had the sheen of the sun on it. She was wearing a simple dress – not coarse like those of the work-ers – but a working dress nonetheless. Louise found her thoughts adjusting to the situation. She remembered Kathenka, the Master's young wife in Delft, who had become like an older sister to her. It was silly to be jealous. Wouldn't it be wonderful if all three of them could some-how co-exist together? In a happier state of mind, she began to scheme.

She knew now that Colette could be touchy. The trouble was that she seemed to have no one she could talk to. Madame Morteau tried hard to be 'Maman' to her, but the older woman seemed to have a genius for saying things that sparked the girl's temper. Colette did seem, however, to have a deep and genuine liking for M. Morteau, and would seek refuge with him among the vines whenever the atmosphere in the house became tense. Perhaps Louise should try to be more like him: patient and understanding, and let Colette come to her by herself?

It was a day or two after Gaston's departure that Colette stood in front of Louise's portrait again. The girl looked shy, almost apologetic, as if remembering what she had said the last time. Louise thought of Pierre and how she had listened to him and silently encouraged him to tell her his problems.

'What were you thinking about, little Dutch girl ... Louise, isn't it? All those years ago. You were asking a question, weren't you? But it wasn't just any old question ... it was about life, wasn't it? And who were you asking? Do you want to know about me?' Louise could feel the girl's hunger for companionship, but it would have to be nursed; acceptance would have to come from her. Let her ask her questions and let her feel that she was answering them herself for the moment. All Louise could do was try to spread about her the warmth of friendship. Little by little Colette began to talk, telling her about Papa Morteau, and how kind he was; how she had an ally in a miller down by the river, but how, otherwise, she was on her own. Madame Morteau still saw her only as a replica of her dead mother, while Margot, though entertaining, was not someone in whom she could confide. There were so many questions Louise wanted to ask, but here in the kitchen there were too many interruptions. She needed peace and time to develop a relationship. Madame Morteau unwittingly came to her aid.

'That old picture is in the way, Colette. Ask Margot to help you take it into the parlour, no one ever goes in there now.'

Louise threw caution aside. 'No!' she said, in silent appeal.

'Colette, ask her to let you take me to your room, please!' To
her relief, Colette took Louise's suggestion as her own and
begged Madame to let her take it. 'It will be company for me
while I am on my own.'

It was a delight to be in the light again after the dark of the
kitchen, and Louise was enchanted with Colette's room. It
was so like her lovely attic bedroom in Delft. She
encouraged Colette to talk to her and the communication
began as naturally and as easily as it had with Pierre. After
all, they were both like shoots from the same vine. The
things that Louise wanted her to ask about were the things
Colette wanted to say. 'Tell me about Gaston, before he
went away,' Louise pleaded. Colette told her of the day he
had sung the 'Marseillaise' and Louise laughed at the image
she created. 'I wish I'd been there,' she said. 'And then he
rode off without even waving goodbye to you.'

Colette stiffened. 'How do you know that?' she
demanded.

Louise, realising she had stepped on thin ice, had to think
quickly. 'I was there when you greeted him when he
arrived, and you reminded him of it,' she said. 'It must have
been awful seeing him go off to war?'

'I wanted to die,' Colette murmured. Then, as if accepting
Louise as an ally, she said more strongly. 'I ran away, you
know. I couldn't stand it here. I had to do something.'

'Tell me,' Louise urged.

Colette began her story. After a while she stopped addressing the portrait. It was awkward having to look up at it from
where she was lying against the pillows on her bed; it
seemed as if she imagined that the girl she was talking to

was sitting in the chair that stood beside the dressing table.

'One minute he was my hero, and next he was riding past swaying in his saddle like a drunken lout. He had said he would wave; that was all I wanted. But he didn't. So I ran away.'

'Where did you run to?'

'Oh, I tried to walk home … '

Louise listened in silent sympathy as Colette told about the journey that led to the terrible discovery of the burnt-out shell that had been her home. Then she spoke of the sense of peace she had felt when she had revived under the cool breeze from M. Brouchard's hat. 'It was like waking to a new life, Louise. I knew then that there was no going back.' She explained how kind M. Brouchard had been to her, but her words were becoming blurred and her sentences disjointed. Louise noticed her eyes flutter and close. Touched by her bravery, Louise bent over her and whispered:

'Sleep well, my little dark-eyed friend.'

Colette's breathing was gentle and easy. Perhaps the relief of telling the story of her rebellion had relieved her; she looked peaceful but weary. But Louise was too charged with energy to fade and spent the quiet hours of the night thinking about her story. She liked the girl. She was glad Gaston had not fallen for some limp flower who would not stand up to him. If she *had* to share him with anyone, then she was glad that it was someone like Colette. But as she watched her sleeping she couldn't help but feel a small twinge of apprehension. No, that was silly, everything was lovely now, she told herself as she pushed it firmly to the back of her mind.

CHAPTER 13

The Winemaker's Assistant

It must have been raining. Louise could catch the astringent smell of moisture on dry ground. A distant roll of thunder grumbled and died away. It wasn't the storm, however, that alerted Louise to Colette's presence, but the way she was moving about the room. Louise had been looking forward to hearing more about the girl's life, but the feeling she got from her now was one of hostility, and these sudden movements made her wary. Colette appeared to be dusting, picking things up and wiping them before putting them down again with a thump. There didn't seem to be any purpose or pattern to what she was doing, she was just 'being busy' for the sake of it. Whenever Louise attempted to reach out to her she encountered an impenetrable barrier. They had been so close the night before; what had happened? Louise was frightened of forcing herself on her new friend, and withdrew like a tortoise into its shell.

She realised that Colette had come over and was standing somewhere near her portrait. The picture frame shook; she was dusting it. Now the duster was passing lightly over the painted surface. Then the canvas shook as Colette gave it a sharp flick with her duster. Louise was taken aback, and felt her anger rising. She had been prepared for Colette to have doubts about her appearing in her room last night, but she hadn't expected her to take it out on her picture. Colette moved away and stood looking out of the window, humming to herself, beating time to the tune with little jerks of her duster, as if she had found the flick to Louise's face satisfying.

'Is that the tune that Gaston sang to the mob the day he went away?' Louise asked, keeping her voice as normal as possible. 'The cadets used to sing it in the barracks in Paris.' Colette's duster missed a beat, then picked it up again; she had heard Louise, but she wasn't replying. Colette began to sing the words, her tightened lips flattening the syllables.

'*Allons, enfants de la Patrie! Le jour de gloire est arrivé ...* ta ta mm mm mm ...'

'I wish I'd heard him,' Louise said. A distant flash of lightning momentarily lit the inky cloud that framed Colette's head. As if the lightning had struck her, the girl spun around to face Louise's portrait, her hands gripping the windowsill behind her.

'Did you appear to Gaston like you appeared to me last night?' she demanded angrily.

Louise was taken aback. Why would Colette be upset by that? Then the reason for the girl's anger struck her like a blow. Her first instinct was to deny any relationship with Gaston and to play for time, but Colette seemed armed for combat; there was no room for prevarication.

'Yes,' Louise responded. 'I sat with him when he was sick, because he asked me to. He had rescued me from a canal, and he had caught a chill as a consequence.'

'And after that? He carried your picture everywhere, didn't he? The boys told me. He kept it in his rooms. Did you appear to him there?'

'Yes.'

'Did he ever ...' Louise thought she was going to say,

"touch you?" but Colette's imagination had led her much further than that. 'Are you … are you his mistress?'

Louise was dumfounded. *His mistress?* Where had the girl got that idea? She was Gaston's friend! She might even admit to being in love with him, but she was not his mistress. How could anyone think such terrible things of her? Stifling her anger, she tried to see the situation from Colette's point of view. Only last night she had sat with Colette here in the intimacy of *her* bedroom. No wonder she was suspicious. And Louise had heard enough talk in the barrack rooms to know that such situations were not uncommon in France at that time. In the Delft of her childhood, loose morals, if they existed at all, were either concealed, or smiled at in 'Merry Company' pictures, where laughing men drank wine and consorted with loose women.

She felt as though her lovely relationship with Gaston had suddenly become soiled. But it had been her fault; she'd been too innocent. And now poor Colette had spent a miserable day wondering if – God knows how – Gaston and she had been lovers. How on earth could she explain?

'Colette de Valenod, listen to me *please* and believe me because you *will* eventually understand. I am not Gaston's mistress, neither in act nor in mind … Yes, I *have* shared Gaston's rooms and his thoughts, just as I am sharing yours now, but I know for a fact that he has never once looked on me with lust or even with attraction above that of friendship.' She realised that this ran perilously close to a lie; Gaston *had* flirted with her, but she recognised now that that was all it was. It was nothing like the feelings he had for Colette, much as it hurt her to admit it.

Colette heard her out, but her face was still sullen, and Louise guessed that she had worked herself into such a state of suspicion that she was just looking for spectres with which to torture herself. Louise tried a different tack. 'There is, however, one girl who Gaston does carry in his mind.' Colette looked up, her eyes flashing. Louise was glad, as sullenness did not become her. 'You would recognise her! She sits under a gnarled old tree looking down into a roadway below; it's as if she's waiting for someone to pass.'

'He was thinking of that?' Colette sounded surprised and pleased. 'He went away without waving,' she whispered.

'Well, that's the image of you he carries in his mind. Was that the last time he saw you?'

'No. He came back for the grape harvest a year later.' Colette's voice was warm with happy memories.

'Tell me about it,' Louise urged.

Colette's face lit up and Louise imagined that same face looking up at Gaston as he rode down the slope, '... the beauty you see today,' he had said. Somehow Louise had found the spring that restored Colette's faith in life, and she began to tell Louise all about that month when Gaston had come home for the grape harvest and love had gone to their heads like new wine.

It wasn't easy for Louise. How she would have loved to have been in love again, as she had been with Pieter, free to laugh, and tease, and joke, and steal kisses as they had high in the Oosterport back in Delft. But Colette's laughter and happiness were too infectious for jealousy to endure. And Gaston wasn't Pieter. He belonged to Colette, and Louise would just have to love him by proxy. They would share him and love him equally in their different ways.

Late that night while Colette slept, Louise thought about the future, and her mind took a more serious turn. Hearing about Colette's love for Gaston had only shown her how deeply she loved him herself. It was foolish to think that they really could pool their affections; three friends together. She had seen Colette's possessiveness, and she had felt her own surge of jealousy. Ultimately one of them would have to yield, and Louise knew which one of them that would be. What would she do then? Retreat into her picture while her friends grew old about her? Allow herself to become an ageless aunt, a ghostly figure hovering on the edges of their lives? No, when the time came she wouldn't linger; she would move on, or just take a different path – to where she didn't know – but she would have to be ready when it came.

She walked over to the window. A full moon silvered the road and the square; nothing moved. Her eyes travelled further, to where a film of mist lay over the river. Above and beyond that was the dark line of the forest, notched at the point where the road to the west snaked out of sight between the trees. Somewhere down that road lay the chateau; she imagined it bathed in moonlight, a fairy castle in a forest glade. The road seemed to be drawing her. She laughed and shivered slightly in the night chill. Colette's flick on the canvas today had reminded her of her picture's vulnerability. Her special box had kept her safe enough while Gaston and the boys were there to look after her, but her picture had nearly been destroyed in the canal, and there wouldn't always be a Gaston to rescue her. Maybe she would be safer in a place where she was not so conspicuous, somewhere like the walls of a chateau, where there were bound to be other paintings?

That might be a path for the future, but for now Louise was determined to live fully in the present. She was prepared to enjoy herself. First she must teach Colette how to bring her with her when she went around the winery and into the vineyards. She thought about her father and how she would have insisted: "tell me *all* there is to know about *everything*!"

Summer was approaching and there was no sign of Gaston returning. The rhythm that Paul Morteau set for the working of the vineyard was based on the calendar of his forefathers. When the French government had announced that the year would now be divided into twelve months of equal length, starting on the day of the declaration of the Republic, the only thing he liked about it were the names given to the months.

Germinal, or 'Seed Time', is followed by *Floréal* , 'The Time of Blossom,' he explained to the vines he was inspecting. 'Don't worry though if you still think of them as April and May, just don't let Monsieur Brouchard of the Revolutionary Committee hear you.' He looked up with a start of mock surprise, as if he hadn't known that his friend, the miller, was standing over him. His little performance over, he said, 'They are a good class this year, *les enfants*; discipline is good,' and he waved an appreciative arm towards the serried ranks of vines that climbed the slope above him. Then he straightened his back and looked over to where the vines that the Count had gifted to his influential colleagues were growing, untended. 'Look at them, the hooligans, completely out of control.'

'Why don't you take them on? Whip them into shape?' said Jean. 'The new owners would pay you, no doubt.'

'No, I won't.'

'Is that wise?'

'Probably not, but one can't make wine from those grapes alone. You see, those vines are not favoured by the sun; they were ragamuffins even before they were allowed to grow wild. However, what is a class without its ragamuffins?' he smiled tolerantly. 'They had their place. One can have too much sweetness, too much culture; in their right proportion those grapes gave our vintage, how shall I say ... its oomph! But the new owners know nothing of this; all they want is to be able to tell their bourgeois guests: "This is the wine from my very own vineyard." No, I will not turn out *vin ordinaire* for them or for anybody. There is only one way that I will make wine for others and that is from the whole vineyard.' He dusted his hands on his trousers. 'But you didn't come up here to sit in on my class. Colette here will mind them, won't you, my dear?'

'*Certainement, Monsieur le professeur,*' replied Colette with a curtsy, and watched the two friends walk down between the rows towards the winery. There they would spend a happy hour among the vats discussing village business. From time to time they would draw a sample up from one of the barrels by dipping in a long tube, sealing it with a finger and then releasing the wine into a tall glass. This they would hold against the light of a candle to judge its colour and its clarity.

'They are a pair, aren't they,' she said as Louise materialised beside her. 'Why didn't you stay? Nobody other than me seems to see you?'

'Oh I wasn't far away, but sometimes I feel uneasy. I think there are people who are more perceptive than others and who might see me, even without my portrait. It feels as if they can pick up the image you are creating for me. Young Pierre is one, and now your Monsieur Brouchard. I really like him, and he likes you, perhaps that's how it happens. It was he who rescued you when you ran away, wasn't it?'

'Yes.' Colette smiled as she remembered.

For a while she continued to tie back tendrils that were blocking the path between the vines. Over the last months she and Louise had become constant companions. Colette had devised a more suitable dress for Louise than her green silk, just as Gaston had thought up a uniform for her so that she could ride unhindered. The new costume was the simple outfit of a country girl: a skirt with a detachable bodice and a blouse of unbleached linen. An apron kept the front of the skirt clean. The sabots that completed the outfit felt to Louise like her native Dutch clogs. If Jean Brouchard had in fact seen her she would have seemed just a typical French country girl with, perhaps, unusually fair hair peeping out from her headscarf.

During the day Louise would be present or absent, depending on Colette's work. As Colette didn't like housework, she had no wish to share it with Louise, but Louise did ask that she should think of her when Margot was around. Margot was their main window on village life. The village sports, however, gave Colette a welcome opportunity to involve herself in a local festival.

'Lucien… Lucien,' the girls chanted teasingly, leaning forward towards their blindfolded hero. 'Give me your last kiss before you're married!'

It had been a day of triumph for Lucien at the village sports. He had lifted and carried the 'testing stone'. This was a smooth and gripless boulder that lay all year among the nettles at the edge of the sportsfield, waiting to be lifted and carried: one ... eight... fifteen... and then today an incredible twenty paces, by none other than Lucien himself. Margot shrugged and pretended indifference. He had gone on to wrestle his way through a field of men and boys like a scythe cutting nettles. Now, because, in theory at any rate, he was to be lost to them through his engagement to Margot, the unattached maidens had started their chant: 'Lucien... Lucien ...'

Margot had explained the rules of this 'imbecile game' to Colette while she broke dishes at the sink after breakfast. At the sports it was customary for any newly engaged man to be blindfold. The unattached girls would line up and the young lover would choose one of them at random for a last kiss before he got married. 'You'll see, it will be that pig Bernadette who will get him! I won't speak to him for a week, I swear!'

'It's a pity you can't be in the lineup yourself. But how will he know which is Bernadette if he's blindfold?'

'Pah! He'll recognise the smell of pig shi– oops!' Colette just managed to catch a second saucer before it reached the floor. She looked anxiously to see if Madame had heard.

'I'll be there, Margot, and I'll see that he behaves. I might even claim a kiss myself!' To her surprise Margot seemed quite shocked.

'Oh no, Mademoiselle, that would never do!'

Sadly, Colette realised that Margot was right. Though she was almost completely accepted by the village now, there was and always would be that small barrier between her and the village girls... but still she would be there!

'I'll keep an eye on Bernadette for you,' she promised.

Jean the pedlar was a regular visitor to the village sports. As no one would make household purchases today, he came with just his donkey cart, laid out with a tantalising array of trinkets, ribbons, sweetmeats and items suitable for the day. One of his treasures was a polished wooden box in which were half a dozen vials of perfume. He would let the girls sniff the tiny bottles and, as none of them could afford a whole one, would allow them a dab on each wrist, and a dab behind each ear, for the price of one sou. Colette, with Louise as an invisible companion, was examining the pedlar's wares on one side of the cart when she recognised Bernadette's voice coming from the other; the girl had a distinctive, rather seductive lisp.

'See what she's buying,' she whispered to Louise. Louise did not like spying, but slipped away and came back a moment or two later.

'Scent ... violets. Jean says it's a new one. I wonder you can't smell her from here; she has bought a double dose for herself. But look ...' Louise broke off, 'it's Lucien's turn to lift the testing stone.' They ran across to watch. The roar of delight from the crowd when Lucien reached the impossible twenty paces echoed round the valley; he was a popular hero. Colette and Louise had difficulty in keeping track of Bernadette in the mêlée of congratulating villagers. It was Louise, however, who saw the moment when the girl bounced up to Lucien, said something in his ear, and then held her wrist up to his nose before she tripped innocently away.

'So that's how he'll recognise her!' said Colette when Louise reported back. She told Louise what Margot had said that morning about Bernadette. They waited until Jean's cart was deserted before Colette approached him. The pedlar wore a hat with a broad rim that covered his beak-like nose. People said he never smiled, but they liked him nonetheless.

Yes, he had a new scent ... violets, would she like to try? Colette explained that the scent was not for her. If she paid for it now, could he give it to someone else later? Then she explained exactly what she wanted. Though his expression never changed, she was sure his eyes glittered under his wide brim. 'I'll see that you get a ringside seat,' she laughed.

The wrestling was over and Lucien was towelling himself down when the chanting began. "Lucien ... Lucien ..." Colette rounded up Margot, who was hissing with indignation like a kettle, to help her. She had no time to tell her of her plan. There was an open space in front of the pedlar's cart. They found the tug-of-war rope and pulled it out to form a demarcation line. Then Colette began to marshal the chanting girls into a line behind the rope, with their backs to the pedlar's cart. They seemed quite happy to have her as mistress of ceremonies. When Lucien had been well and truly blindfolded, Colette shuffled the girls in the line, making sure that Bernadette was near the end. They were too occupied entering into the fun to notice that Colette had preserved a gap in their line by the simple expedient of leaving her hat on the ground. She looked beyond it; Jean the pedlar was there, feeding his donkey on a handful of oats and rubbing her soft nose.

Now the whole crowd was taking up the chant. Two of Lucien's friend held him by the arms to ensure that he didn't touch the girls until he had decided which one was to receive his coveted last kiss. A hush fell on the gathering. He was facing the first girl in the line. Lucien was entering into the spirit of the game; he strained forward as if they were having to hold him back. The poor girl in front of him was in such a lather of embarrassment that she only just managed to whisper the prescribed words: 'Kiss me kind sir,' before she dissolved into helpless giggles.

'Alas, I have only one kiss to give, and it is for another,' Lucien declared.

'Watch him breathe in!' Colette's whisper was lost in the derisory comments that met this declaration. Lucien's minders moved him on. The next girl in line would clearly have given her new bonnet for Lucien's kiss. He drew in a deep breath, which he then skilfully transposed into a sigh of disappointment, and she too was passed over. Another unfortunate, and then came the gap in the line that had been faithfully preserved by the presence of Colette's hat. Lucien's minders were moving him past it, when Jean the pedlar's donkey suddenly took it into her head to step forward and join the parade. There was a snigger from the crowd. Colette shushed it hastily. Lucien's two minders, sensing fun, pushed him forward just as if he was in front of the next girl in line; the donkey obligingly raised its head. Colette noticed Lucien breathe in. She saw from his smile that he had smelt something. Everyone was waiting. Had two sous worth of scent been enough, she wondered? Could he be smelling donkey as well? Another breath, still no action. Then, to her dismay she realised that she had forgotten that someone would have to say the magic words. Where was Louise? She turned and therefore missed the moment when a girl's voice, seeming to come from the donkey itself, said: 'Kiss me, kind sir!'

That was Bernadette's voice surely, even down to her charming lisp! Lucien's response was immediate. He stood up, his smile widened under his blindfold, and he announced for all to hear: 'You, fair maid, will receive my last free kiss!' With that, he swept the blindfold up from his eyes and found himself gazing down into the interested face of Jean the pedlar's donkey. They said afterwards that the roar of delight from the crowd could be heard in Auxerre, but that was impossible!

Lucien stepped backwards in surprise. He made to turn, but his two minders had him firmly by each arm. They had both been trounced by him in the wrestling ring less than an hour ago, and he was not going to get away without delivering his promise. Jean came forward with a palm of oats. While the donkey nibbled, Lucien, still dazed and puzzled, bent and kissed it on its velvety nose. He stiffened; he sniffed, nose down on the donkey's face.

'Now then, just one kiss, my boy,' someone shouted. But a broad smile was spreading across Lucien's face, then he put his head back and roared with laughter.

There were many sore ribs from laughing that night, and many a sore head from the party that followed. For the moment however it was Margot who led Lucien from the field in triumph, while Bernadette swore silently that she would still get her kiss.

The events at the village sports gave Colette and Louise plenty to chuckle about when they went back to work in the vineyards. When not working among the vines, Colette would move to the wine cellars where the massive barrels stood in rank. Louise would examine the presses and the vats while Colette made up the records. They spent long hours in Papa Morteau's attic office. While Colette struggled with the accounts that had not been properly kept for years, Louise would gaze out over the vineyards, watching the clouds spreading and withdrawing their shade over the regimented vines. Colette would show her the figures and explain how the resources of the vineyards were being quietly bled away by the Count's 'generosity'.

'If only we had the management of the whole vineyard again, I … we could satisfy everyone's needs.'

It was, however, the process of making wine that really fascinated Louise. She was a silent observer while Colette and M. Morteau discussed the progress of their vintages and what to do about them. She soon noticed that the vigneron listened seriously to Colette's suggestions, even deferring to her opinion occasionally. Colette would glow then, and Louise would want to hug her, realising how proud she was of having M. Morteau's good opinion.

Louise often found herself thinking how her father would have enjoyed all this. But he, like her, would have been looking for scientific answers to what was going on. He would have wanted to know what was happening inside the vats during fermentation. What made crushed and pressed grapes froth and foam when nothing had been added? Annie, her old nurse, would sometimes add rising dough from the baker to get her country wines bubbling. Was there a connection between dough and grapes? Colette seemed unable to answer this sort of question. Was M. Morteau just being kind when he praised Colette's work?

One day Louise lingered among the vats while Colette went to rinse a glass, and found herself alone with M. Morteau who, unconscious of her presence, continued the discussion he had been having, but addressing the wine they had been tasting.

'She's right you know, you *are* musty, you old rogue. We'll have to get you out of that barrel. I'm beginning to think she has a better nose than I.' Then, with a change of voice, he went on a little sadly. 'What would I do without her? I have gained a treasure but I seem to have lost a son.' He sighed. 'It would be greedy, I suppose, to want both.'

Louise, feeling she was eavesdropping, moved away. Even so, she stored away what he had said. When the time was right, she would tell Colette how much he valued her. She watched as he moved about, talking to himself, and found herself thinking about Gaston. For the first time she saw Gaston's likeness in his father. Not the efficient soldier – that came from Madame – but the gentle Quixote that hid behind Gaston's moustaches, the soldier who did not want his two cadets to be turned into barbarians. Dear Gaston … when would he be back?

As summer came, Louise and Colette filled Gaston's absence by talking about him. Louise held nothing back, unless she felt that she might be betraying his trust. They talked and planned together, engaging in an imaginary future where there was no rivalry between them and they would never grow old. Not for the first time since Gaston had given her an independent existence Louise wondered if she had a purpose, a reason for being here. Was there anything she could share with Colette?

One day when thinking about M. Morteau and his wines, Louise remembered standing on the walls of Delft, her home town, watching Pieter. He was gazing out over the fields, his eyes partly closed, seeing the cloud shadows with an artist's eye. Then she told Colette about Delft, and the Master, and Pieter.

'M. Morteau is like them, Colette. When he calls the grapes his "children" and his wines his "class," he is like Pieter trying to see the essential lines, colours and lights of his subject. How I would love to go back in time and

introduce you to Pieter and the Master. It was he who predicted that I might live again if someone – like you and
Gaston – had the eyes to see me. Do you think your wines
have their own sort of life after death? Ask him for me
Colette, please!'

It was evening when Colette and M. Morteau were walking on the track that ran round the periphery of the vineyard, gratefully catching the late breeze that was being
sucked out of the valley below, and Colette put Louise's
question to the vigneron.

'Papa, tell me, when the moment comes and we hammer
the cork into one of one of our bottles, does the wine die?'
M. Morteau stopped, obviously surprised, but pleased too.
He took a moment to think.

'No, Colette it is not dead, it is just waiting. All the beauty
is there, but it has to be released. The wine we make,
Colette, must hope for someone who has the palate to bring
it to life in all its glory.'

'But how do you know that it will be appreciated? Don't
you long to run after it and say to the man with the cork-
screw: "Hey! Stop talking … look… taste… savour… enjoy!'

'Oh yes!' he laughed. 'But be warned, that's when we start
drinking our own stock.'

Colette seemed to be about to say something more, but
Louise put a finger to her lips. After a pause he went on.
'Colette, you and I grow grapes here on these slopes and
make wine in the winery below. We put our skill, and not a
little of our souls into the wines. But we can't follow them
when they leave our gates. We have to trust that they will
represent us faithfully; they are our ambassadors. We can't
control the situations in which they will find themselves. All
we can do is hope that some of them will find a palate that

will understand our message, maybe for a moment of cele-
bration, or to ease a hurt, warm a heart, or stiffen the resolve
of someone who needs it.'

For some reason this simple statement brought tears to
Louise's eyes. Was that what she was: an ambassador? Had
the Master had such faith in her?

CHAPTER 14

Seeing Double

Ever since he had rescued her, Jean Brouchard had gone out of his way to be kind to Colette; indeed he almost regarded her as a daughter. Colette told Louise how, when things had gone wrong between her and Madame, she used to come down and sit in Monsieur Brouchard's noisy little office and tell him of her woes. He would say little, but would send her home feeling comforted. Then, sometime later, she would see him talking to M. Morteau among the vines, or surprisingly, find him sitting uncomfortably in the parlour with Madame, nursing a small liqueur in his huge hand. Then things would mysteriously improve and, for a while at any rate, Madame and she would be friends.

August was ready to merge into September when Lucien brought a message from M. Brouchard saying that it was a long time since he had seen Colette, and could she drop down some time soon. So she and Louise set off armed with a small basket of eggs from Madame, whose hens benefited from the grain-rich sweepings of the mill. Louise had her own reasons for wanting to visit the mill. Apart from the prospect of seeing Lucien showing off his muscles for Colette's benefit – he might be engaged but that hadn't robbed him of his eye for a pretty girl – the whole mechanism of the waterworks enthralled her. She had been inside flour mills in Holland when they rocked, swayed and groaned as the sails of the windmill swept around. In the water mill, however, the power was contained under the mysterious control of the sluice gates that channelled the water into the mill-race.

Colette had agreed to ask M. Brouchard, on Louise's behalf, how he adjusted the speed of the mill. He was surprised at the question; Colette hadn't shown an interest in the mill before. But as he demonstrated how he could raise and lower the sluice gates to get the right flow into the mill-race, she nodded with well-assumed interest. When the demonstration was over they moved into the little office. Louise, forgetful of the miller, stood behind Colette for a moment, stooping to whisper her thanks in her ear. Something made her look up; M. Brouchard was staring directly at her.

'Excuse me, Mademoiselle,' he said rubbing his eyes. 'But I seem to be seeing you twice.' He laughed uneasily. 'Two Colettes are undoubtedly better than one … but perhaps it is a trick of the light.'

Louise stood frozen, not sure whether to move or to stand still. She had been careless; he really did have the eyes to see her. He looked away, shaking his head as if to dispel the double image, and Louise moved quickly out of the dusty sunlight that haloed Colette where she sat. He seemed relieved when he looked again.

'So, you have seen how I work my mill. Now tell me, how are things up at the winery?'

Louise never ceased to be surprised by Colette. She had seen her cross swords with Madame, her eyes flashing, just as she remembered her own father's eyes flash when he was roused. Then again she had watched her happily discussing some 'truant' vine with Papa Morteau as if the unfortunate plant was standing in front of them, cap in hand. Now she was giving M. Brouchard a detailed account of the woes of the winery, complete with acreages and yields, even figuring the dire effect on the business of the Count's generosity with his land and his gifts of wine. The miller sighed.

'And how is Paul taking all this? When I talk of these things he goes to earth like a worm before a thrush.' Colette smiled and then frowned.

'He's worried. He was forced to lay off a few of the workers ... he hates that.'

Brouchard nodded. 'I know.'

'He won't say things straight out, so sometimes I don't know whether he is talking to his vines or to me. I think he feels that something evil has crept into the valley and that the dividing of the vineyards is just a symptom of this.' She stopped, wondering if M. Brouchard would understand.

'I'm listening, my dear. Paul Morteau is one of my oldest friends; he can sometimes see things that we poor plodders and grinders just don't see ...' He thought for a moment; "Something evil" you say. I wonder ... ?' Then he changed the subject: 'Now, tell me how things stand with Madame's cousin, the Count. Has there been any progress in the negotiations to buy the land that is her due?'

'No, as you may have heard, the family have refused to meet his price.' Colette's shoulders drooped – no land, no Gaston. M. Brouchard got up and went to the door, touching her shoulder in sympathy as he passed. He opened the door, looked up and down, then closed it firmly.

'Mademoiselle Colette, I asked you to come down to talk to me, but I haven't yet told you why. I need your help, but in order not to deceive you, I have to tell you some things that *must* remain secret between us.'

'Even to the family?'

'Yes, even to Gaston. You see, there are times when it is safer for people not to know the whole truth.' Colette nodded; she understood this very well.

M. Brouchard began, stroking his beard forward from underneath as he did so. 'There are rumours, yet to be confirmed, that the Count – *"Citoyen du Bois"* as he now likes to be called – is involved in plans for a royalist uprising similar to those taking place in Normandy and Brittany.' Colette's eyebrows shot up, but she didn't say anything. 'Any day now I expect to hear details of the exact time and place of a meeting of the conspirators. Duty tells me that I should give this information to the authorities so that the Count and his friends may be caught and brought to justice. If we can prevent this rebellion, countless innocent lives will be saved. Whatever about being brought to justice, the Count must be stopped!'

Colette realised that the miller was looking at her as if needing confirmation that there was no alternative to stopping the Count. She nodded; another rebellion would be intolerable.

The miller sighed. 'Now for my dilemma. As the Morteaus do not own the winery or the land, if anything happens to the Count, not only will they be ruined, but the winery will close and the whole economy of the village will collapse. Everything I have striven to maintain will be lost. My report to the authorities will be like poking a stick into a hornet's nest. The army will be upon us, and with them will come the politicians, the spies and the inquisitors. No one's life will be safe then: not yours, not mine, not the Morteaus'. The Terror works by terror, and I have sworn to myself to keep the guillotine out of this village. The Count knows this; he has me over a barrel.' He cocked his head, listening, out of habit, to the grumble of the mill wheels above.

'You have a plan, or you wouldn't have asked me here. How can I help?' Colette asked.

'I have a plan, yes, but like a chain, it is only as good as its weakest link. My plan is that the Count du Bois should receive a visit from a certain distinguished Lieutenant of Hussars.'

'Gaston?' Colette queried. 'But ... that would have to be official, wouldn't it? Poking the hornet's nest, like you said?'

'As Chairman of the Revolutionary Committee, I have certain privileges. I am authorised, for example, to ask for a small detachment of horsemen to be sent to investigate a rumour of spies in my area. I know the colonel of Gaston's regiment and will make the request through him, asking that Gaston be the officer in charge; after all, he knows the area. I will say nothing about the Count or the information I have about a meeting. If all goes to plan, it will look like a routine patrol. If Gaston happens to find that his cousin, the Count, is in cahoots with royalist insurgents, I think we can rely on him to send them packing and to scare the pants off the Count in the process. Gaston will simply report to his superiors that some rebels have been routed. No inquisitors, no trials, no guillotine.'

'I'm sorry, M. Brouchard, but there are several reasons why this plan could never work. The first is that Gaston would never spy on the Count – they are cousins after all. The other reason is that, if Gaston did find the Count plotting with the royalists, he would feel honour bound to treat him like any other traitor, and turn him over to the authorities. I know Gaston, you see. So the whole house of cards would come tumbling down anyway.'

The turbulent sounds of the working mill filled the room while the miller considered what Colette had said. Finally, he gave an exclamation and slapped his hands on his knees, raising two little clouds of dust.

'In that case,' he said, 'it is up to us to persuade Gaston to re-open negotiations with the Count *before* the meeting takes place. Colette, my dear, this is where you come in; between us we must persuade Gaston that he owes it to his family, to the village, and to you, to secure the future of the winery, no matter what the cost to his pride.'

Colette had known that this suggestion would come and had been dreading it. It was a family secret, but it would have to come out now.

'Monsieur, Gaston won't go. You see, it is not just that he let it be known that the family have refused to pay the Count's demand. The fact of the matter is that they can't. M. Brouchard, the coffers are empty.'

The miller leant back in his high chair, looking as if he had been hit.

'Aah! So there are no funds. And I thought it was just Gaston's pride. What has happened to their prosperity; they used to be the envy of us all?'

'The Count has been bleeding the winery for years. The vintage records are perfect, but sadly, no proper accounts have been kept.'

'Oh, my friend Paul. No wonder you slid away from me when I asked how things were going.' He looked at Colette. 'But you are keeping accounts now, aren't you?'

Colette's modest shrug told it all. 'It makes no difference. When the Count's letter came, they counted everything: the money's not there.'

Brouchard put both hands under his beard and pushed it up so that it made a fearsome thicket in front of his chin. 'So, there is my weak link. You came to our village too late, my dear.' He closed his eyes and sighed … 'I had hoped to kill two birds with one stone: stop the Count and secure the land. Now I have no alternative; I will *have* to call in the authorities. God help us all.'

Above their heads the millstones continued, pulsing out their own distinctive rhythm. The stones seemed to be talking to Louise, forming words in her mind: louder and louder. *Now's the time* they rumbled, *now's the time.* She tried to plead with them: *No, not so soon! Not so soon!* She felt like a prisoner whose date of execution has unexpectedly been brought forward. *I want more time, I want more time,* but she had no more time. Colette was getting to her feet. *Now or never, now or never,* the millstones ground urgently, and Louise knew that if she didn't act now she might never have the will-power to do so again.

'There is always my portrait,' she said, loud above the din of the mill, 'the portrait of the girl in the green dress. It is worth the price of this land, I believe.' Even the dust motes that hung in the air stopped moving. She had given no thought to how, or even whether, M. Brouchard would hear her, but her message was for him. Colette began to turn, but then, afraid of revealing Louise's presence, froze. Her mouth opened and closed as she struggled to contain her protest. But Louise had eyes only for the miller, who was standing, like someone trying to recall a dream. Then she saw his face clear as if he remembered what it was.

'You know… that picture that Gaston brought back in the spring, does he still have it? It was standing in the kitchen for a while. A girl in a green dress, if I remember?'

'Yes?' Colette's voice was a whisper.

'One of his cadets told me that an expert in Paris said it was worth a small fortune.'

'Oh, but Gaston would never, ever, sell it!' Colette exclaimed. Her voice dropped, 'And I … I'd hate to see it go.'

'But it could do the trick, Colette … it would be something to bargain with. Gaston could go to the Count with his head up, and all we need to do is let him make a courtesy call to the chateau with his troop, a day or two before the meeting, and no one need know that he is renegotiating. If we get the timing right, he can make the Count accept the picture as security until he can raise the money. His presence alone will scare the Count into cancelling the meeting. I *have* to keep the guillotine and the tumbrel out of the village, Colette, and this could be our only chance.'

Put like that, all Colette could do was to nod and allow him to usher her dumbly to the door. 'Lucien will bring up a bag of grain for Madame's chickens,' the miller said, as he rubbed his hands with satisfaction, and watched fondly as Colette walked up the road from the mill. Then, for a moment, he peered intently after her, shook his head, gave it a thump with the heel of his hand and muttered, 'I'm sure I need glasses.'

On the walk back to the winery Colette was furious with Louise for having 'sacrificed herself' as she put it, and then with herself for having agreed with M. Brouchard that there was no alternative.

'But it *is* the answer, Colette. There is no alternative,' Louise comforted her friend. 'It will be only for a little while, you'll see.'

A week later a covered cart smelling deliciously of apples drew up at the mill. The apples, picked green from trees in Normandy a few weeks ago, were packed in barrels. Beside these were wooden boxes with cheeses carefully laid out in sawdust. M. Brouchard selected a fine cheese for the house, and then sent Lucien to his wife with a basket of apples for winter storage.

'So, you have been following them?' he asked the driver once they were ensconced, glasses in hand, in the privacy of his inner sanctum.

'As well as I can. They are keeping to the forest tracks where no one will question them. I told you about their disguise?'

'You did indeed. Clever.'

'I lost them for a while when they skirted Le Mans and had trouble again after Orleans, trying to guess where they would intersect the road. There was a troop of hussars in the area.'

'Are you quite certain that they are aiming for the Chateau du Bois?'

'Yes. Fortunately one of their boys is partial to our apples. They have great hopes of your Count, but this is as far east as they intend to come. They call themselves 'les Chouans', after the calls their boys use to signal in the forest. They will move back west then and try to attract more waverers to their cause.'

'The folly of it,' sighed M. Brouchard. 'Just more peasants killed for a lost cause. You say we can expect them to be at the chateau next Wednesday?'

'Yes, this day week. The boy seemed certain of the date. Their disguise dictates the speed at which they can they travel.'

Jean Brouchard opened the flap of his desk and took out a small cloth bag, weighed it in his hand, and then passed it to the man. He would have liked to have talked more, but the matter was now urgent.

'There's a bit more here than usual, *citoyen*, because I am going to ask you to keep this to yourself. I think you will agree that there are times when it is best to clear up one's own mess rather than let others do it. If you are headed north, though, I will ask you to deliver a letter for me.'

'Certainly, *citoyen*, and thank you; these days, there is not much profit in apples.'

One of the places where Louise liked to sit was in Paul Morteau's light-filled office looking over the vineyards. She would perch on the edge of a table, where she could see out, and at the same time listen as he and Colette discussed the small daily matters of the vineyards. She felt secure here and M. Morteau never gave any indication of being aware of her. Several days had passed since their visit to the mill, and the glow of self-sacrifice that she felt when she had volunteered her picture to save the winery had faded. After the homely life of the winery, the prospect of the chateau seemed bleak. What would she find there, other than the silence of empty rooms? Her only role would be just to be there as a guarantor of Gaston's debt. Her reverie was broken when Paul Morteau straightened himself up, and pushed his spectacles high on to his forehead; he had been updating his planting plan in tiny writing.

'Jean Brouchard was in this morning, Colette. He told me that he wants Gaston to trade his picture of the girl in the green dress, to buy Maman's portion.' He turned to look at

Colette as if to see her reaction; she made a slight shift of her shoulders. Then he said in a low voice: 'You'll miss her, my love, won't you – this girl who is your friend?' It was Louise who started. She glanced at Colette who, in turn, was gazing at M. Morteau, her mouth moving as if she was trying to find appropriate words.

'How...?' she said at last, 'How do you know, Papa, can you see her?' He smiled and shook his head.

'No, sadly my eyes don't work that way, or perhaps I just don't have the skill. But when I saw you talking to yourself in the vineyards, I thought that you had caught my habit of talking to the vines. Suddenly you laughed. Of all the attributes I bestow on my grapes, a sense of humour is not one. Perhaps I should try; a sparkling white wine with laughter in it would be nice, wouldn't it? I guessed then that you had a companion, even if I couldn't see who it was. I had not seen you happy since Gaston went away, and I wondered who or what it was that was amusing you. Then I remembered the portrait, and how you had asked for it in your room. If anyone could walk out of the frame, that girl could. Then this morning, I found poor Jean complaining that he had been seeing double when you were down at the mill, and was sure that I was right.'

'Yes, Papa, you *are* right. Her name is Louise and I will miss her terribly.'

'Of course you will, my dear. We love the things we have made, our creations; they are part of us. Just think, you have done exactly what the artist who painted her would have hoped, just as I hope that my wines go to the palate that will bring them to life. But we have to learn to let them go when the time comes. My great temptation is to go on tasting my wines, for the pleasure of reassurance. But I did not create these for my own pleasure. If I drink for pleasure I will lose my palate; I wouldn't be the first to succumb to drinking my own stock. When my wines are ready, much as it pains me, I must say, "You are finished here; now, you must go out ..."'

'... and be our ambassadors?' Colette finished for him, with a small smile.

'Yes, they have their own purposes, but they need their freedom, and our trust, to make it happen.'

Their voices went on but Louise was quietly repeating to herself the word: "Purpose!... purpose?" When she was little and had been good, Annie, her old nurse, would tell her that that was God's purpose. Annie had assured her that God was guiding her every step. But she and Annie's God didn't seem to get on. Under His guidance, she seemed to trip and end up flat on her face. So with the help of her father, she had turned to science instead.

But the purpose that M. Morteau had been describing didn't come from outside. What if her real purpose was inside her, rising like a spring, bubbling up from every facet of her existence? Father's friend Spinoza had talked like that. She thought of Mother, Father, Annie, Pieter ... she had been nourished in life by their love in so many ways. Then there was the Master, who, in complete trust, had hurled her forward into the future, where she was now. M. Morteau had talked of his wines as ambassadors; she could be an ambassador for all those people who in their different ways had fed her with their love.

Louise emerged from her thoughts and heard M. Morteau explaining:

'You see, Colette, Jean Brouchard and I have our own

ways of understanding the valley, and what goes on in and around it. He takes the facts, and mills them down until he finds the truth. But country people don't always think that way, so when they come to me they tell me stories. We walk among the vines and things emerge that they could never admit to Jean, possibly even to themselves. They will seldom openly accuse a neighbour, because they all have skeletons of some sort in their cupboards. So they fall back to the old folk tales, stories of witches, magical happenings, and hoards of gold. Sometimes they talk just to lay their own ghosts, but sometimes they tell me things.'

'And this time?'

'It emerged as one of those standard tales about a monster and a maiden in distress, but I teased at it, pulling out threads from the story until I could fit it to a real life situation. It transpires that a new housekeeper has been appointed to the chateau. With her has come her daughter, a very pretty child of about thirteen, described to me in terms such as "Hair like spun gold" etc etc. For some reason the locals are worried about the child. I suspect they are unhappy about the behaviour of someone on the estate and feel that the girl is at risk. That's all I can get out of them, no names, no hints.'

'And you think that if Louise was in the chateau she could help?' Colette asked doubtfully. 'But who would be there that could give her life? She mustn't be in any danger, or I won't let her go.'

'No, indeed, I can't conceive that any harm could come to her. Like the best of ambassadors, I suspect that her presence will be enough.'

That evening Louise felt very close to Colette. They had heard that Gaston would arrive tomorrow. Their paths would diverge then, and her picture would pass on, perhaps forever. She had one more task before she went, but that must wait for Gaston.

Gaston's small troop, wearing cloaks to disguise their uniforms, arrived by the same route that he and Louise had followed in the spring, slipping quietly in at the gates of the winery. They could advertise their presence when they knew what would be required of them. Gaston's orders had read simply that a small band of insurgents had come into his home area: *Further information will be supplied by the Chairman of the Revolutionary Committee.*

Margot heard them first and ran to the door, followed in quick succession by Colette and Madame Morteau; even being quiet, eight men and horses make their share of noise. Orders were called, hooves scraped, steel clashed on steel, and when they shed their cloaks, it was as if exotic poppies had suddenly flowered in the yard. Madame thrust the girls aside and stepped forward as Gaston, still cloaked, handed the reins of his horse to a trooper, and strode up to embrace her.

'Mother, how are you. We have been posted here for a few days. Will it be all right if my men occupy the bunkhouse?'

'Of course my son, but ...'

'Excuse me, Mother, I will explain later; I am required to see M. Brouchard without delay.' Gaston stepped back, saw Colette and Margot crowded in the doorway, bowed stiffly, turned on his spurs, remounted his horse and rode out of the gates. Louise felt Colette stiffen with indignation, and was amused and sympathetic.

'Don't worry Colette, that's how he behaves when he's playing soldiers.' Colette had a lot to learn.

Gaston rode slowly through the village, his leisure studied, smiling and nodding to people he knew. Once he had got this interview over he would think about taking some leave. He wanted to see Louise and ask her what she thought of Colette. He tethered his horse in the loading bay of the mill, and went in search of M. Brouchard, eventually finding him and Lucien working with chisels to deepen the grooves on the upturned mill wheel.

'Gaston! My friend,' cried the miller. 'Here, give me a hand up.' Gaston pulled him to his feet. 'Home for a little while, then? Nice to see you.' He slapped him on the arm. 'We must celebrate. Lucien … finish this off if you please.' Down in his room he helped Gaston off with his cloak. 'I'm so glad you've come. If your colonel had sent me someone else I think I would have pretended it was a false alarm – a small domestic matter.' As he talked, he fished under his desk and produced a bottle of brandy and two small glasses. 'Here's to business, *santé.*' They clinked glasses.

The millstone was disabled and the only sound was the swish of water falling from the paddles of the water wheel, so they were private enough. M. Brouchard dismissed talk of royalist insurgents as probably insignificant, though, as there was mention of the Chateau du Bois, he would like Gaston to call out there tomorrow to see that the Count was all right.

'What is really concerning me, however, is the ownership of the winery…' If Colette had been listening, the words '*wily old fox,*' would have sprung to her mind. It wasn't long before M. Brouchard had so loaded Gaston with moral responsibility for the welfare of the village and its people

that he would willingly have sold the clothes off his back if
that would have made up the price of the land that would
'save them all'.

'Now, Gaston my friend. Tell me about that picture you
brought back from Holland ...'

As M. Brouchard showed Gaston to the door, he suffered a
small pang of conscience. He had told Colette that he would
send Gaston to the Count a day or two *before* the proposed
meeting of the rebels. In the end the temptation to have
Gaston burst in on the meeting and find the Count and the
rebels in cahoots had proved too much. Because Gaston
might have scruples about spying on the Count, he had of
course told him nothing about the rebel meeting. Soldiers are
used to surprises and Gaston knew enough about the
dangers of official involvement to deal with the situation
discreetly and on his own. Brouchard's pang of conscience
was that he hadn't told Colette about the change of plan, but
perhaps it was for the best; she would only worry.

It was with a heavy heart that Gaston rode back to the
winery in time for the evening meal. How could Brouchard
know that a painting he had pulled from a canal in Holland
mattered more to him than all his other possessions put
together? How could he explain to Louise that he was going
to sell her?

Over dinner in the winery the family talked about the
weather, how the grapes were coming on, and Gaston's
journey from Auxerre. Then, as if to fill a gap in the conversation, Madame turned to Colette and said:

'By the way, Colette, I told Gaston's two cadets to take
that picture that's been cluttering up your room and clean

the case up for Gaston.'

Colette was flabbergasted. Gaston looked apprehensive. 'But Madame, it is perfectly clean ... You mean you sent them ... but that's my room!' The thought that they had gone in and just taken Louise without asking her was an affront. What would Louise think?

'Oh, don't worry, my dear, Margot showed them up. They won't have disturbed anything.' Colette's anger was rising like milk about to boil over. She had been bracing herself for Louise's departure, but not like this. Her room was her refuge. She looked at Gaston for support, but he wouldn't meet her eye. She turned back to Madame, guns ready to blaze, but saw Louise standing behind Madame, one finger to her lips. With a monumental effort, Colette got herself under control and turned away.

Gaston cleared his throat. 'Listen, everyone,' he said, straightening his back. 'I must explain something. I am persuaded that we owe it not just to ourselves but to the village to secure the future of the winery by buying your portion, Mother. When I was here in the spring and tried to work out a way of raising the money it seemed that we had exhausted every possibility. However, there is one item that I overlooked.'

Madame threw up her arms. 'What can that be? We have no gold, no secret hoard?'

'It's something that none of us has considered, Mother. It is the picture of the girl in the green dress.'

Madame Morteau started. 'The picture? But surely it cannot be worth that much? *Mon Dieu*, and I got those boys to take it!'

'You needn't worry, Mother, the boys have guarded that picture since the day I took it out of the canal in Holland.

They are far more of a danger to themselves than to it. And, yes, it is valuable, very valuable. Pierre overheard an expert who examined the picture in their barracks in Paris give it a price. It is worth a small fortune.' He paused and looked beyond his mother's head to where Louise stood. 'It was never my intention to part with her, but we have responsibilities. I will take the portrait to the Count tomorrow and offer it, at least as security, until we can raise the money.'

As Colette gazed at Louise, tears began to move slowly down her cheeks. What would she do without her friend? Madame was struggling with her own emotions. She felt a little ashamed. She had been jealous of the portrait, perhaps because she had sensed that it had provided Colette with the very things she had been so unsuccessful in supplying: love and support. M. Morteau looked uncomfortable, as he always did when there were suggestions that he should become a landowner. Louise's eyes were fixed on Gaston, who was staring, not at her now, but at Colette. Perhaps it was the tracks of the tears on the girl's cheek that were affecting him, perhaps it was her look of vulnerability, but if Louise had still harboured ambitions for Gaston for herself this would have been the moment when she would have given them up.

That evening, after everyone else had gone to bed, Gaston and Louise sat alone at the table in the dining room. He had retrieved her portrait from Marcel and Pierre immediately after dinner. Louise thought that this might well be the last time that she and Gaston would sit like this, quietly talking. Tomorrow they would ride off together, but that would be a different chapter in her life. So they reminisced, going over all the things that had happened to them, and all the things they had done together.

'I will come and get you back Louise, as soon as I have the money,' Gaston promised.

Louise shook her head. 'No, Gaston, you don't understand. This is the price I have to pay for the fact that you have given me life; it's something I didn't want to accept, but I must, and so must you. I am a point in time, Gaston, created by you from the Master's portrait. I am sixteen years old, and I will always be sixteen years old. I can't grow old with you even if I wanted to; it is you who will move on.' She wanted to hold him. He seemed vulnerable and lost. 'Colette loves you, Gaston, and I love her almost as much as I love you. When I think of you both together I feel brave enough to face the future ... but that future is not here. There is no room for three in the practicality of love. And with Colette you have all you need. Gaston, you have no idea of the quality of that girl!'

Colette had gone to sleep worrying that Gaston and Louise might be in danger when they rode off tomorrow. M. Brouchard had said, that day at the mill, that he would send Gaston to negotiate with the Count before the meeting of the insurgents took place, but there had been delays, and yesterday the miller seemed to be avoiding her when he came to talk to Gaston. In the end she went to sleep, realising that there was nothing she could do about it.

Sometime later she woke, feeling that Louise had called her. She looked around the bedroom for the painting. Then she remembered – it was below in the kitchen. She put a dressing gown about her shoulders and lifted her hair so that it fell in a dark cascade over the collar. Moving silently, she slipped down the stairs and stood hesitantly at the bottom. Gaston and Louise were talking, heads together. For an instant she felt betrayed, excluded from their *tête-à-tête*. Then she realised that they were talking about *her*. Louise was telling Gaston how wonderful she was and how she had almost taken over the running of the winery. She stepped down and interrupted them.

'Don't listen to her, Gaston, she exaggerates most terribly.' Louise stopped in mid-sentence, and they both turned to her.

Gaston's jaw dropped. 'Colette! You mean you can see Louise ... like I can?'

'Of course she can. We've been friends all summer!' Louise laughed. 'You see, Gaston, you're outnumbered.'

Gaston, clearly bewildered, managed a bow. 'I yield to fairer forces,' he said gallantly.

Louise beckoned. 'Come, Colette, please.' She rose to her feet. 'You have both been seeing me in the clothes you devised for me. As this is a special occasion, I want to wear my green dress. So please, both of you, concentrate hard on my portrait, and I will come back to you.'

A hundred and forty one years previously, Pieter and the Master had gasped in appreciation when Louise shed her cloak and the green silk dress had cascaded about her. Now, both Gaston and Colette took an involuntary step towards her as she stepped forward. Wouldn't it be wonderful, Louise thought, if Pieter and the Master could be here to see the effect of their creation?

'My dear friends, the one thing that I find unbearable about going is leaving you behind. How can I live without ever having gone through the grape harvest with you, Colette, and how will I see all those wonderful places and interesting things that we were going to see when we rode together, Gaston? I ask just ask one thing. Think of me at the grape harvest, and if you have to go back to war, Gaston, think of me when you see something beautiful, or curious, or grand. I can't be certain, but I hope that I will at least know that you are thinking of me, and perhaps even see something of what you are seeing.'

Louise held out her hands, one to each. 'On the day when my portrait was conceived,' she explained, 'there were three of us in Master Haitink's studio: the Master, Pieter and me. The moment came when the Master had finally captured the image that you see in my portrait, and he slumped forward with exhaustion. Pieter and I hurried to help him to his feet. Then for a moment we all three stood like this holding hands in a circle.'

Colette and Gaston could never remember precisely when it was that Louise was no longer there, because that was the moment when they both discovered that they had no other wish in life than to be holding hands with each other here alone in the kitchen of the winery of Les Clos du Bois.

CHAPTER 15

Charcoal Burners

It was mid-morning before they set off. They had discarded their cloaks; M. Brouchard had said that their uniforms alone would act as a deterrent. As far as the troop was concerned they were on active service so strict discipline was imposed. Marcel and Pierre rode within the troop where Gaston could keep an eye on them. Ever since Pierre had challenged Marcel, there had been friction between them, and Gaston liked to have them under control. Written orders had come for him that morning; he recognised General Bonaparte's seal, but chose not to read them until this day's work was done. The letter lay unopened in his sabretache, the pouch that hung beneath his sabre. He felt annoyed with Brouchard for putting him under pressure to close a deal with the Count, and devastated at the thought of losing Louise, but in his heart he knew it was the only thing to do. Louise's portrait was packed in its box and strapped to the remount they had brought from Auxerre. It restored Gaston's feeling of gallantry to be giving Louise an armed escort.

The forest had once been well tended, but now ancient and tired oaks dipped mistletoed branches close to the forest floor. The carriage road played tip and run with a stream that still carried last year's leaves on a final twirl back down towards the valley. Louise had decided she could join

Gaston, and she sat straight in her saddle as she rode silently beside him.

'I am glad you've come,' he said. They rode in silence for a while. 'You know that this is not what I want, Louise, but thank you for what you did for us last night. Colette has told me about your summer together; I wish I had been there. I never realised how awkward the situation has been for Colette at home. I will talk with Mother, she really wants to love her, you know, but somehow they seem to spark off each other.'

'The best thing you can do, Gaston, is to come home, both for Colette and for the family. She needs you. She understands the business and she understands your father, but without you she has no authority.'

Gaston grimaced. 'It may not be as simple as that. I got orders this morning, I haven't opened them yet ...'

'Bonaparte? I recognised the seal.'

'It is not possible these days to leave the army simply because you feel like it. Conscription is general for all but the wealthiest. But whatever happens, I swear I will try to get you back from the chateau.'

'I don't know if I *want* to go back, Gaston; I don't know *what* I want. The explosion that killed me cut me off before I had a chance to experience life, to become a woman. I feel I am incomplete. Now, I'm torn between wanting to go back to my old life and to Pieter, and wanting to go forward, to see if there is completion for me there. I chose reality rather than heaven because I loved the world, but I'm only now realising the cost of love. I must go on, Gaston. You will secure your land, and in time you will get my picture back. And there may be something I can do in the chateau; your father has given me a small commission—'

'My father?' exclaimed Gaston, but before Louise could answer, an ear-splitting call rang out from somewhere near them in the forest.

'Holy God almighty! What was that?' Gaston stared about him. A more distant call answered the first. He turned to his troop. For some reason Pierre had pulled up without warning, causing Marcel to rear his horse. Gaston could hear the corporal growl with irritation as the troop crowded to a standstill. Suddenly all discipline seemed to break down. The troop was backing off; the two boys were circling each other. To his horror and fury Gaston saw the flash of steel. With a roar of anger he spurred his horse down on them, drawing his sabre as he rode.

Order was restored. The two cadets, disarmed and flanked by a trooper each, sat on their horses, heads bowed.

'Now, Cadet Colbert,' Gaston said to Pierre. 'It was you who pulled up without warning. Why? Have you never heard a wildcat before?'

'With respect sir,' Pierre said in a low voice, 'It wasn't a wildcat, it was a call like us lads in Normandy use when we are in the forest, sir.'

'Speak up, Colbert! You mean it was human? Did the sound mean something, then?'

'Yes, sir...' said Pierre, encouraged, 'we use calls like that during the mock fights we have between our villages, sir. That call sounded like a warning, sir, like when a rival gang is coming into our territory... Sir... Marcel called me...'

'Forget about Marcel. That's an order! But what in God's name are boys from Normandy doing here in Burgundy?'

'Sir ...?' Pierre wasn't sure if he still had licence to speak. 'Could they be Chouans?'

'Chouan rebels, you mean? I suppose it's possible. Good

heavens, Chouans, who use the call of an owl – *chat-huant* – as a signal. Perhaps there is something in Brouchard's rumours then. What did the call say?'

'I didn't catch it all, sir, but it ended with the words "in the chateau."'

'Well, well, I wonder if my precious cousin is in trouble?' Gaston sat and thought, his horse shifting her feet contentedly in the leaves. 'Our orders were to look out for "spies", but I must admit I never quite believed in them. Do you think that shout will have warned the people in the chateau?'

Pierre nodded. Louise could see that he had forgotten his disgrace and was already vibrating with excitement. This was a game he understood.

Gaston continued: 'It would be useful if we could keep the leaders in the chateau while we take a look.' He stared at the eager face of the boy in front of him. 'All right, here's a chance for you to redeem yourself, Colbert. Listen carefully, we'll try it this way.' Pierre's face lit up.

Louise moved away. So ... Brouchard had said nothing to Gaston about the Count's plot, and neither apparently had Colette. Could it be that the meeting was actually today? Louise smiled to herself; Brouchard was no fool.

The soldiers were busy tying Pierre to his horse, albeit loosely. Pierre's 'escape from captivity' was sudden and dramatic. Stripped of his shirt, and with his hands still apparently tied, his horse burst from the knot of soldiers and headed straight for Louise. A shout went up from his 'captors'. Hands reached out to grab him and a sabre flashed in the sun as they wheeled about, deliberately getting in each other's way. For a terrifying moment Louise thought that Pierre was going to ride straight into her. She heaved at her reins to get out of his way. For a second, as he thundered past, their eyes met. Then he was gone, but the flash of recognition had been there. Soon, from the woods behind her, she heard Pierre's triumphant call and her hair stood on end. It was a wild feral utterance made more eerie by the fact that there appeared to be human words embedded in it. Gaston was making a convincing show of anger with his men, calling back the chasers and barking them back into squad formation. There were other calls now, near and far, but it was impossible to say where they came from. The party rode on, with Gaston riding clear, leading his troop from the front, as he liked to do. Louise, having recovered from the confrontation with Pierre, rode up to join him. She wanted to hear what he was planning.

'Pierre is telling the lookouts that we are the first of a much larger force that is spreading out through the forest to catch them. But he will tell also them that the chateau will not be searched because the caretaker is a renowned Jacobin.'

'Will Pierre be all right?' Gaston didn't answer, but she saw the muscles at the angle of his jaw bunch up.

'Please, Louise,' he said. 'I must concentrate.'

She had to bite her tongue. After about half a mile the forest ahead grew lighter and the road forked. Gaston reined back and checked the priming in his pistols as his men rode up. 'Corporal, I want you to take your men to the right here. That will bring you past the front of the chateau. Don't even look in the windows; as far as you are concerned, the house is empty. Make plenty of noise while you spread your men out, then set off, as if to search the forest to the west. Beauchamp and I will investigate the caretaker's entrance at the back.'

'What about other entrances, sir?'

'We will have to take a chance on those. They should still all be closed with the government seal. The only reason the Count, sorry – "*Citoyen du Bois*," is there is because he's wangled himself the job of caretaker. He'll want to preserve those seals at all costs. Give me five minutes, and then double back. I want the chateau surrounded. I don't know how you will do it with just eight men, but that's how I want it to look from inside.'

Gaston watched the soldiers move off. Then, beckoning to Marcel, he took the fork leading to the rear of the chateau. They kept to the soft margin of the road so that their horses' hoofbeats were muffled. Gaston wasn't aware of Louise following, but guessed she was there. As they passed a small woodsman's hut the scent of freshly cut logs filled the air. At the back of the chateau, farm buildings extended out, facing into a courtyard accessed by a high stone arch. Gaston saw that the heavy wooden doors stood open, and leant back in his saddle to murmur to Marcel.

'They must have someone to relay the calls inside, so look out for the messenger. I'll take care of any guard they have set.' Over the chateau roof they could hear the corporal cursing his men into line. 'Come on!' Gaston drew his pistol and spurred his mare forward. The horse's hooves slipped on the cobbles beneath the arch. He had to steady her, trying at the same time to scan the yard. Two once fine carriages were drawn up. Their horses, tethered nearby, were still nosing hay that had been recently forked out for them. What drew Gaston's attention, however, was a covered cart; the cart itself, its horse, and even the buckets and baskets that hung beneath it were black. Even as he wondered what that might mean, he caught the unmistakeable smell of old burned wood. Of course – charcoal burners. But what on earth was his cousin doing entertaining *charbonniers?* Surely they weren't inside? The back door, the caretaker's entrance, stood ajar. Perhaps his arrival had already been reported? Gaston leaned forward and rolled from his saddle. He landed on his feet, a pistol ready in his hand. Leaving his mare to look after herself, he ran for the door. As he did so there was a sudden flurry behind him and two objects shot past him, converging in a tangle of arms and legs at his feet. One was Marcel, the other a child of about twelve, his features soot black from charcoal. Gaston had no choice but to leap over the struggling pair. As he did so, the mounting wail of the boy's warning call was cut short; Marcel had clapped his hand over the lad's mouth.

'Damn, he bit me!' Gaston didn't wait to sympathise; if he paused now, he would lose the element of surprise. He had been to the chateau before. He knew the way: down the corridor, through the kitchens, past a baize door. He tiptoed across the tiled hall to the door of the banqueting room – still no guard. He listened and could hear a murmur of voices inside.

'Cousin,' he murmured, 'Are you keeping bad company, or are you a captive?' Controlling his breathing with difficulty, he eased the door open. Light streamed in at the partly curtained windows and reflected off the vast mahogany table. He could see papers and maps strewn across its surface. He waited for his eyes to adjust to the bright light. There were eight men, all with their backs to him, staring out between the curtains, craning forward to see the last of the soldiers disappear into the forest. He felt carpet under his feet and slipped silently in. In a second they would turn and see him. He raised both pistols.

'Don't move gentlemen, and don't touch anything on the

table.' Their heads turned as one; only two of them reacted with speed, sidestepping so that Gaston had to adjust his aim, while their hands dipped to their pockets, revealing where pistols were concealed. Gaston covered them immediately. 'Raise your hands! I didn't realise that charcoal burners carried pistols these days.' Without taking his eyes from them, he eased the flints on his pistols back to full-cock. They, at any rate, would know that his triggers were now on a hair. 'Pistols on the table please. One at a time.' They placed their weapons on the table and stepped back. Gaston looked at the pair with interest. Their disguises were perfect down to the last detail, only the pink of the hands that they had washed, presumably to handle the papers in front of them, betrayed them. Gaston was impressed, what perfect cover! Charcoal burners – always a law unto themselves – migrant workers who moved through the forests, different but not alien, would never be questioned. The eyes that challenged him now were not, however, the eyes of woodsmen. Gaston had seen such faces before, gentlemen perhaps, but also fanatics. His determination hardened against them. It was people like these who, for their own ideals, had been leading poor peasants in their thousands to certain death.

The rest of the party were a strange mix; five were in the motley garb of gentlemen who were doing their best to look like ordinary citizens. He recognised several of them, members of the local aristocracy who had evaded prison and the guillotine by slipping into the mass of the citizenry and declaring openly for the Republic. He had to smile at the incongruity of these once mighty men doing their damnedest now to look insignificant. In complete contrast to all of them stood his cousin, the Count du Bois. Here, in the apparent safety of his home, he had donned a wig over his peasant crop, put on an embroidered coat, and even sported the hated culottes and silk stockings of his class.

Louise had slipped in behind Gaston and now surveyed the gathered company. The two ragged charcoal burners were a mystery to her; she would have to ask Gaston about them. The others, though they had the manners of gentlemen, seemed unnaturally self-effacing. It was the Count that caught her eye. His elaborate clothes drew her attention, but it was his face that held her. She could see a family likeness between Gaston and him. He was older than Gaston, of course – about forty – but strikingly handsome in a way that both attracted her and repelled her. For all his relaxed suavity there was something predatory about him.

'Gentlemen,' the Count began. 'What a fortunate coincidence. Do let me introduce my cousin, Gaston Morteau, a lieutenant now, if I'm not mistaken? My congratulations on your promotion, Gaston,' he gave a reassuring smile.

For a moment Louise was taken in by the voice, the smile and the hypnotic reasonableness of the Count's delivery. Then, with a start, she remembered where she had heard such a voice before. It was the one Reynier DeVries had used when taunting Pieter on the steps of the hidden church in Delft. Reynier who had deceived her, and everyone else, with his easy charm while he schemed and lied in order to get her fortune for himself.

She could feel Gaston's resolve wavering, just as hers had wavered under Reynier's thrall. It was as if the Count had invoked some ancient feudal bond that Gaston could not deny. Like the poison from a spider's bite it was spreading through Gaston, paralysing him.

She had to warn him. But she dared not distract him by

speaking. She threw her mind behind her thoughts, and willed him to hear her.

'Don't listen, Gaston, it's flattery. Watch out!'

Her warning worked. Gaston literally started out of his trance. For the next few minutes, while Gaston argued with the Count and the company, she prompted and supported him, their thoughts flashing silently back and forth faster than any lip or voice.

'I don't think names and introductions are necessary, Gaston,' the Count declared smoothly.

'Why no names?' Louise asked.

'They are Royalists, Louise. He is protecting them.'

'So the Count's declaration for the Revolution means nothing!'

'Nothing, he's a traitor.'

The Count turned to his visitors. 'Gaston has come about a small family matter, gentlemen. Forgive us if we talk together for a moment or two. Shall we retire, Gaston? Obviously it would be nicer to do this over a bottle of our splendid 1790 vintage.'

Gaston kept his place and his silence; the Count countered with a graceful shrug. 'Your gun is really quite unnecessary, my boy. You see, since I wrote my last letter to you, it has been on my mind that it is time that I allowed your dear mother the opportunity to exercise her marriage option. I'm sure we can reach an amicable arrangement?'

'Oh, Gaston, yes! If you accept, then we can all go home!'

Louise forgot her own resolve.

'Don't tempt me, Louise.'

'But this is what everybody wants! The house and vineyards would be saved, you could get out of the army and come home.'

She couldn't quite bring herself to say, 'and marry Colette'.

She heard Gaston say, 'And the price, Monsieur le Comte?'

'My dear boy, not a louis, not a sou. I have given enough to the Revolution to feel nothing but satisfaction at giving to my own family. All you have to do is to walk out of this room, mount your steed, follow your gallant men into the forest and forget everything ... *everything* ... that you have seen here.' The Count's smile was confident and reassuring.

Louise didn't care whether they were republicans or royalists. What did it matter if this motley bunch went free?

'Go on, Gaston, accept it.'

Then she heard, through Gaston's mind, as distant as a dream, the voices of the noyades – not the defiant cry for the king – but the pitiful voices of despair as the water rose about the prisoner's necks.

'Louise, I can't. These men are plotting civil war! It is not their lives that matter, but the lives of all the innocent people that they will lead to certain death!'

He took a deep breath. 'Thank you, cousin. You know where my heart lies.'

Immediately the tension in the room relaxed. The Count had played his cards well, the young lieutenant was as corruptible as the next man; they could breathe again. Then Gaston went on: 'Let us review the options, gentlemen. If I accept, I become complicit in your conspiracy,' he smiled and shrugged, 'but then what's another corrupt officer in an already corrupt regime? I will gain property and status for my family, and all at no cost. If on the other hand, I refuse, I sign away not just my family's rights but their dreams and livelihoods as well.' He laughed. 'That's a high price to pay for my honour.' He had let his voice drop, as if accepting his own moral defeat.

The conspirators were exchanging secret smiles. Suddenly Gaston spoke out, and the menace in his voice was palpable.

'Well, *Citoyen du Bois,* I refuse your offer. And if you have any doubts on the matter turn and look out of the window. The chateau is surrounded. There is no escape, either from the chateau or from me!'

Involuntarily they all turned and looked out to where horses were coming and going, clearly on organised business. The corporal was obviously doing a thorough job as commander of his imaginary battalion. Gaston took advantage of the diversion to draw the two surrendered pistols to his side of the table.

One by one the company turned back from the window and took their seats around the table; seeming to have lost the power to stand. Only the Count maintained the pretence of nonchalance, sitting back from the table, swinging a stockinged leg.

'What will you do now?' Louise asked Gaston.

'Guillotine the lot of them!'

She winced, doubting that he meant it, but it was a slap on her hand for having tried to tempt him; she wouldn't interfere any more.

Gaston spread his hands. 'Gentlemen, my duty as a soldier is fulfilled. I have no doubt that on this table there is enough evidence to put you all under the guillotine. I will, of course, arrange for our Chouan friends to be shot as spies if they prefer.' He paused. 'However, I have a proposal to make.'

The Count looked up in surprised expectation. 'You, cousin,' Gaston addressed him. 'You offered me what I most sincerely desire – house, land, and future – not out of generosity on your part, but as the blood price for your own head and those of your companions. You can keep your land. My demand is on a different scale altogether.'

He turned to the two Chouans. 'Last year I witnessed Frenchmen killing Frenchmen, not in tens, not in hundreds, but in thousands. And why? Because you and your like led those innocent, ignorant peasants to their doom for your own ends. I will not stoop to killing you, my own country-men, without offering you a choice.'

'Between the guillotine and a firing squad, I suppose?' said one of the Chouans mockingly. Gaston's manner became factual and impersonal.

'I will take all the evidence that I see in front of me on this table and I will hold it hostage against the behaviour, not just of you as individuals, but of all of you collectively. You will swear an oath that none of you will ever again take up arms against your fellow countrymen for any cause, neither will you induce any one else to do so. If one of you betrays his oath he brings the rest of you to justice.'

He turned again to the two Chouans. 'I am fully aware that my evidence against you will be of little effect once you have passed out of this region. However, I believe you to be men of honour and therefore to be relied on not to break your oath. But think long and hard before you swear.'

Louise watched, fascinated. Had Gaston read his men correctly? The two Chouans were struggling with their con-sciences. Sweat cut pale rivulets through the charcoal on their faces. Finally they exchanged glances of resignation. Louise breathed again, Gaston was right. These men's per-verted sense of honour would never let them break their oath.

'Now, place your hands on your hearts and swear.' The

five local conspirators could hardly get their hands to their hearts quickly enough. The two Chouans dropped their heads, but their words were clear.

'We swear.'

It was only later that Louise realised that she hadn't seen the Count's lips move.

Louise thought that she never would understand men. The group who only seconds earlier had been looking at certain death were now apparently relaxed, laughing – in relief perhaps – but still laughing.

'Tell me, Gaston,' asked the Count. 'Why did you come here? Did you know I had visitors? Or was it to beg for your land? Surely you haven't been able to raise the price I asked?'

Louise could feel Gaston weakening. *'I can't do it, Louise, I can't sell you like some … some concubine.'*

'You are not selling me, Gaston,' she responded. *'This is my choice, so I give myself. Don't think about it any more, just give him my picture – now.'*

The Count's eyebrows were rising in an elegant arch as his question remained unanswered.

'On the contrary, I *can* meet your price,' said Gaston, 'and have indeed come to buy our land.' Everyone was alert again; there was just a frisson of tension in the air. Could this in some way let them off their oath? Gaston continued, 'While on active service in Holland I had the good fortune to acquire the company of a young lady of beauty and breeding.' There were knowing smiles in the company. 'Unfortunately, the roaming life of a hussar is not a suitable life for such a refined young person. In return for the land that is

our due I plan to make over this young lady to you, cousin.'
The Count glanced at his friends; he sensed a trick, at best a
joke, but he wasn't sure.

'May I be introduced to this young lady?' he asked.
Gaston moved to the door, opened it a crack, and called out.

'Beauchamp, kindly hand in Mistress Louise, will you.'
Marcel was back in a moment. He handed the case to
Gaston who took it from him and firmly closed the door on
him. Gaston set the case down on the table, and carefully
freed the painting. 'Count, I think some of these gentlemen
are familiar enough with great art to affirm that this picture is
full and adequate payment for our land.' Gaston turned the
picture around and placed it on a chair facing his audience.
'Gentlemen, let me introduce Mistress Louise Eeden.' There
were murmurs of appreciation, and a sharp intake of breath
from one of the charcoal burners.

'Oh ... what a gem!' he said. 'The Dutch School. I have
seen pictures in Holland that are so perfect that you feel that
you could walk into them, but this one is special. Look, it
is as if she is about to step out.' He laughed with delight.
'Monsieur le Comte,' he called, 'I do declare this little lady
must be worth more than that potter's field you were offering the lad. Come Count, where will you hang her?'

In the hubbub that followed, Louise slipped over to
where Gaston was quietly sweeping the papers off the table
and putting them into the empty picture case. She felt a
sudden pang; the boys had had that case made for her back
in Holland. She wanted more than anything now to stay
with Gaston, to take to the road with him again, or go back
to Colette and the grape harvest that she had never seen.
She watched sadly as he tightened the straps. While the men
were hanging the picture in pride of place beside the

chimney, Gaston passed the case out of the door to Marcel, with instructions to guard it with his life. He had just returned to the table when the Count hurried over. For once the suave aristocrat was having difficulty in expressing himself.

'Gaston please, I ...' then he blurted, 'I can't take your picture.'

'Why, what do you mean? You have no choice.'

'I don't want her ...'

Louise was amazed and a little hurt; there were beads of sweat on the Count's forehead. He was plucking at the lace on his collar.

'Don't you like her?'

'Oh, for God's sake!' the Count snapped. 'She's captivating, but there is something about this picture ... even I can see that. I don't trust myself with it. Take her away and you can have your land, I don't want anything for it. I can see that this girl has cast a spell on you. This Louise, is she a witch?'

Gaston turned on him: 'How dare you! Look, cousin, I've had enough. The currency for your escape from the guillotine is honour, not gold. You know full well that the only thing that will keep these men's swords in their scabbards is respect for their oaths. If you refuse my payment, the land you make over will become a bribe. My honour will be in tatters and they will be free to do as they will. Keep your "pieces of silver". You will take this lady and you will treat her with honour and respect, but I warn you – she will watch your every move. Should you deviate from your oath in any way, you will find out the sort of power she has!'

For a few precious minutes Gaston and Louise stood close together, looking out of the high windows. The trees were still green but it was the mature green of late August. The Count had left to assist the gentry and the charcoal burners with preparations for departure; outside, the besieging 'army' was looking a bit ragged.

'How will you explain all of this to your soldiers?'

'I'll say that the meeting here was innocent. It was to discuss agriculture in order to ensure that sufficient wheat is planted on the old estates so that the people don't go hungry. The charcoal burners have as much right to demand hospitality as any citizen, but I'll instruct Marcel to escort them out of the region; the catcalls were just boys being boys.'

'Is Pierre safe?'

'I'm sure he's fine. He's among his own, and his wits are quick enough as long as he doesn't have to kill anybody. He'll talk his way out of any trouble. You'll see, he's no fool.'

'Don't go, Gaston.'

'What! It was you who insisted you had to stay here. I have to go.'

'No, I meant don't go off on another mission. I know you carry new orders in your sabretache, but now that you have bought the land, why not stay and help your father and Colette in the vineyard?'

'I wish I could, Louise, but I am bound by law and oath to serve my country. These orders will make it impossible to resign my commission. Remember that the vineyards are reduced in acreage through what the Count has given away; my mother's portion is small, and my soldier's pay will be needed at home. I will leave the army when I can, with honour. I don't think Colette would enjoy the life of a hussar, as you did.'

Louise looked out at the beaten grass. 'I will miss Pierre. I think he saw me in the forest, you know, when he escaped.'

'Perhaps it's best that you stay, then. I'd be jealous of him!'

'Keep him away from Marcel.'

'This is Marcel's last mission with me, I promise.'

Louise turned to him, her eyes brimming with tears. 'So this is goodbye, Gaston. But you take my love with you. Remember me – now go. Go quickly before I change my mind.'

CHAPTER 16

Le Jacquot

The clatter of hooves, the jingle of harness and the shouted orders that had been Louise's life since Gaston had rescued her from the canal, faded and were gone. Her tears spent themselves gradually and the silence of the chateau wrapped her around.

As the power of Gaston's presence began to fade, she felt her picture calling to her as home calls out to the tired traveller. She would soon merge back into the canvas. Now she stood beneath it and took what might be her last long look at the Master's creation. She thought of him; those were his brush-strokes there, and she smiled as she remembered him in all his moods: prickly, teasing, arrogant, kind. Her eyes wandered about the 'room' he had conjured up for her, turning one corner of his attic studio into a sumptuous study for the purpose of the painting, full of things that reflected her interests: books, music and science. There was the Turkey carpet that Pieter had painted so beautifully. She closed her eyes and tried to recall every feature of the attic studio: the light that fell in coloured segments through the stained glass, the great cupboard and the rich smell of the paints. She recalled the different objects of wonder among the clutter at the end of the studio that the Master kept as props for his paintings: the stuffed birds, the suit of armour that the Master had once put on for her benefit. Then she remembered the little laboratory beyond the clutter, and suddenly there was Pieter, standing over his brazier, with his back to her. He was so real that she cried out, 'Pieter!', then threw herself forward, hurtling down the tunnel of time, back to the boy she loved.

She could see him now, a tiny figure in the distance, just as she had seen old Claes through the wrong end of her father's telescope. Oh, she wanted him with every fibre of her being, not just her mind but in her body as well. In a second they would be in each other's arms. She was running; Pieter had turned, he had seen her. His face broke into his broad familiar smile, but then his expression changed to one of alarm. He held up a hand, palm outwards, as if to stop her. Louise looked down. The ground below her feet had dropped away. An abyss, too wide to cross, had opened at her feet, and she teetered on the edge, her arms back to keep her balance. A cry of desolation and anguish escaped her. In that moment she realised that she might never be able to retrace her steps to him. Surely she deserved a second chance; Pieter was so close, so close.

The ground was wet as if from a recent shower. A low sun broke through the clouds: instinctively she looked east, away from the blaze of light. How many times had she seen just such a passing shower sweep over the flat fields of her native Holland. There it was, the expected rainbow forming a bridge that arched over the chasm. With a shout of joy she ran towards it. Annie had always told her that angels could pass up and down to heaven on a rainbow; surely she could cross over it to Pieter? But then she heard her father's voice – the voice of the scientist: 'Louise, my love, you can never find the foot of a rainbow,' and she faltered. If she made that crossing she would have to abandon the reality she had

chosen when she had lingered over the shattered town of
Delft. She would never find out what happened to Gaston
and Colette, never ensure that the Count kept his promise.
All that she had done in this time would be set aside. The
Master and Pieter had created her for the future, that future
was here and now. If the rainbow had a special meaning for
her it was not that she should follow the footsteps of angels.

For an age Pieter and she reached out vainly towards
each other in one long silent cry. When their arms grew tired
they dropped them and simply gazed. Then at last they
turned away and Pieter watched as Louise began the long
climb back to the present in the Chateau du Bois, carrying
nothing but a memory, like an unresolved chord in a minor
key, and a longing that only imagination could fill.

For over a hundred years the picture of Louise had hung
forgotten or disregarded in the back rooms of Delft. The
silence that she had experienced then had been the silence
of oblivion, a dreamless awareness of self, but nothing
more. But here, in the chateau, she seemed to be aware of
every sound. As the temperature in the room changed, the
wood of the oak panels would yield elderly sighs, quite
unlike the snaps of the young wood she remembered from
their new house in Delft. There were insect sounds too, and
the patter of mice. A wasp buzzing out its life in a spider's
web at the window filled the great room with sound. Then
in the distance, she would hear voices: doors would close,
and feet approach, only to recede into the distance again.
Sudden rain hammered at the windows, and then as the
cloud rolled on, light would flood the room again. She had
expected to fade back into her picture as she had done

before, but some energy was keeping her here. Occasionally she would slip into dreams from which she would emerge with the feeling that she had been somewhere else, that Gaston had said something amusing, or that Colette had just left the room. Next time, she decided, she would 'stay on' in the dream, in the hope that her friends were closer than she thought.

It was Colette who showed Louise what these dreams really were. Louise watched as a series of vaguely familiar shapes gradually came together, then detail began to emerge just as detail is added to a painting. She realised that she was looking out of M. Morteau's window at the vineyards spreading up the hill. Was this a memory? No, there were piles of baskets at intervals up the slopes; she'd never seen the grape harvest herself so this must be real, this must be now. Then, quite clearly, she heard Colette's voice.

'I'm thinking of you, Louise, just as I promised I would. Do you hear me?'

'Yes, oh yes. I can hear you!' Louise said out loud, but her voice seemed to be no more than a whisper dissipating in the space around her. She shouted, 'Colette!' but heard nothing in reply. Desperately she reached out with her mind with all the love and intensity that she could muster, and in return heard Colette respond.

'Louise, I feel that you are close. Tomorrow the grape harvest begins; you always said you wanted to see it. I promise that I will think about you whenever I can. Gaston will be home too; we will think of you together.'

For the next weeks Louise was treated to a kaleidoscope of impressions as both Colette and Gaston, true to their promise, remembered, and reminded each other: "Louise would love to see this ..." And so she saw the treading of the grapes and heard wild gypsy music in the evening. Louise was always hungry for more, but there were many times when they were both too busy to give her a thought. Also there were times when Gaston and Colette were private together, and their thoughts were turned in on each other. What she experienced then was neither pain nor joy, but a mixture of the two, and she would draw herself in, like a snail into its shell.

Then, one day, when the grape harvest had been over for a week or more, Louise found herself looking at Gaston from behind. He was in uniform, on horseback, and riding up a steep cobbled street. Surely this was the street up to the castle in Auxerre? But who was giving her this view? She could see a horse's head rising and falling in front of them. This couldn't be Colette; the harness was cavalry harness. Gaston, looking very gallant, had just pulled up his horse and was smiling down at a group of prettily dressed girls who were crowding around him. They were joking, asking him for something, but yet nervous, poised like a flock of small birds, ready for flight.

'Mesdemoiselles,' she heard him laugh. 'I would have kisses for *all* of you, but you see, my cadet is watching, and he knows that I am recently engaged to be married.'

'Ohhh,' they chorused in mock disappointment. Then, they wheeled about like swallows changing flight, and turned their attention to the rider behind. At last it dawned on Louise that the rider must be Pierre. Dear Pierre, was he really thinking about her? At that moment he lost his nerve with the young ladies and clattered up the hill behind Gaston. So, Gaston and Colette were engaged? They could have told her, but … she gave a sigh. This was how it would have been if they had stayed together. It was natural that they should be thinking of each other and not of her.

With the reassurance that she was still remembered, Louise learned to let go at night and drift into an energy-conserving sleep so that she could be alert and aware during the day when her friends might think of her. Only one thing happened to disturb her routine, and it always happened at night. She would feel some powerful source of energy drawing her up from the depths. Then, rising like a swimmer emerging from a deep dive, she would see a light widening above her. As she broke the surface, the light would disappear, and she would be left, charged with energy, to wonder who or what had called her. The only thing that connected these incidents was the state of the moon; on each occasion it was full, and she was grateful to be able to see that the room was empty and she was on her own. The only clue to a previous presence was the heavy scent of pomade that lingered in the air.

A golden tinge had crept into the light. Autumn was passing, and le Jacquot, the log boy, small for his fifteen years, came into the great hall to light the fire. The routine had started a week earlier when the partly drawn curtains had been pulled back, and the room flooded with welcome light. A matronly woman armed with a feather duster had stood back from the windows and was viewing the spider webs with distaste.

'Marie!' she called. A girl of about thirteen appeared in the doorway.

'Maman?'

'Call le Jacquot, Marie. This room feels musty. From now on we will have a fire in here once a week to keep out the damp. Tell Jacquot to get one started. Then you can come and do some dusting.'

'I'm not going to dust while le Jacquot's here!'

'And why not?'

'He's just the log boy.'

'If I hear any more of your fine talk, young miss, I'll smack your bottom. Off now and call him.' The girl flounced out of the room, but almost immediately she could be heard happily calling *"Où est le Jacquot ... le Jacquot?"* till the baize door to the servants' quarters closed behind her.

The room felt warmer now and the air was sweet with the scent of wood-smoke and fresh logs. Jacquot was standing back from the cavernous fireplace to see that his logs had caught from the blaze of kindling below them. He had brought hot coals in a bucket from the kitchen to get the fire started, now he heaped on a few dry logs from the pile stashed inside the wide chimney breast. Late evening sun was streaming through the tall windows and straight onto Louise's portrait. The boy looked up and their eyes met. Louise, who had been only vaguely aware of his presence up till now, felt the electric tingle of his gaze. The Master had been right; there was no telling who would have the eyes to bring his picture to life. The boy involuntarily pulled off his cap and murmured, 'Mademoiselle'. At that moment a voice called from the door.

'What are you doing, Jacquot?' Young Marie was standing there. The boy scratched his head as an excuse for having taken off his cap while the girl skipped towards them. He blushed at her presence. He stood a good head higher than she, but he was clearly in awe of her. Louise thought how pretty she looked in the warm glow of the evening light, her face tilted up to him.

'Do you like me, Jacquot?'

'*Oui*, Mademoiselle Marie.'

'Will you kiss me?'

'*Non*, Mademoiselle.'

'*Pourquoi pas?*' She was indignant. Why not?

'Because it is not my place, Mademoiselle.'

'*Oui*, Mademoiselle... *non*, Mademoiselle... I am Marie... Jacquot.' He was looking at the floor. The girl looked up past him and noticed Louise's portrait. 'Who is that?'

'I don't know, Ma'm ... M... Marie.'

'I see her name! It's painted on that vase thing. She's Louise.' Then the girl asked, 'Can *you* read and write, Jacquot?'

'*Oui*, Marie,' the boy said uncomfortably. '*Pardon* ... I must go.' Marie watched him pick up his bucket of ashes and his empty log-basket. When he'd gone she turned to Louise's portrait and smiled, then she put out her tongue at her, and skipped after Jacquot out of the room.

Louise came to look forward to Jacquot's visits and to watching young Marie's innocent attempts at seduction. She was an engaging creature and Jacquot clearly liked her, but something was wrong. They would appear to be happy together, then Marie would say something, or perhaps move a little too close to him, and he would back away. It was as if a shutter had dropped between them. One day Marie lost her temper with him, calling after him:

'Le Jacquot, you are a clod, a country bumpkin! And you smell of trees!' Louise remembered how Madame would bring Margot to heel by referring to her loudly as 'la Margot', the servant. She could see now that 'le Jacquot' could be just as effectively used. When the boy had retreated, head down under her blast, the child turned to Louise's portrait and said in a meditative voice:

'Jacquot … you know, I don't think he's a log boy after all; he is really a handsome prince in disguise, condemned to live alone in a hut in the forest to the end of his days. Perhaps a kiss from me is all he needs to be released from his spell, like in the fairytale? Oh, why won't he let me near him, what is he afraid of?' And she wandered from the room, for once disconsolate.

Louise felt genuinely sorry for her, but also vaguely disturbed. Then, deep inside her a memory stirred, and she was alert. It was the child's reference to a fairy story that had reminded her. She recalled M. Morteau's concern about a young girl who might be in danger at the chateau. He had wanted Louise to 'keep an eye out for the child …' It seemed absurd, what danger could she possibly be in? Jacquot looked harmless, and she hadn't been aware of another male about the place. If only the Count could have been an ally – but no – there had been something predatory about him; he made her shiver. The idea of being an 'ambassador' had been attractive when M. Morteau had mentioned it first. But what on earth could she do? When Colette and Gaston were on hand, acting on her own initiative had seemed entirely possible. They were her hands and eyes; now she just felt helpless.

Marie did not appear on the evenings when Jacquot came to bank up the fire and make sure that all was safe for the night. When he had done that, he would stand in front of

Louise's portrait for minutes on end, holding a candle in one hand, exploring every inch of the room that the Master had created for her. Finally his gaze would come back to her and linger on her face. He had not spoken to her since his startled 'Mademoiselle' that first day when their eyes had met, but Louise felt that he was wondering about her rather as someone will wonder if the ice on a canal will hold their weight. She waited.

Her first surprise came when Jacquot arrived to bed down the fire, concealing a book under his jacket. When he had finished making the fire safe he placed his candle on the mantelpiece, checked that the door was closed, and took up the book. As if solely for Louise's benefit, he began to read aloud, slowly at first, his finger following the line.

'*Cendrillon* – as told by Charles Perrault,' he started. Louise was enchanted by a story of a fairy godmother who had enabled poor Cendrillon to go to the King's ball, and how the prince – who had fallen in love with her – identified her by the glass slipper she had dropped when midnight struck. Each week Jacquot read her another story from his book. She was horrified when the wicked wolf threw himself on Little Red Riding Hood and 'gobbled her up'. She laughed at Puss in Boots, and was satisfactorily horrified by Blue Beard, who systematically murdered his wives. Some of the stories she had heard from Annie, but Annie's endings were always very moral. Louise gave up wondering how it was that a mere log boy like Jacquot could read, or even why he should choose to read to her. In the end she just enjoyed the stories.

One evening she noticed Jacquot behaving nervously. He went several times to check that the door was closed. When he opened the book, she saw that, this time, he was reading from pages that he had concealed inside the covers. Had he found some new manuscript? Lousie watched his fingers as they followed the words, and remembered her own early efforts with a pen. The telltale marks of ink were on his first and second fingers. Surely he hadn't written this himself? While she listened to his now familiar voice, she had an uneasy feeling, as if she had forgotten something, something that this story was to remind her of ...? Her unease lasted only a few seconds, then she was caught up in his tale.

The Wood Boy and the Monster

There was once a just and a noble king whose castle stood in the middle of a great forest. He was loved by all and feared by none. Close to the castle walls there lived a boy, who made his living by cutting wood to burn in the castle fires. The boy had scarce seen twelve summers when his mother died, leaving him an orphan.

The king, taking pity on the boy, put it abroad that he should be allowed to eat in the castle kitchens, and gave orders that his chaplain should teach him his letters. When however he commanded the boy to leave his cottage and to take up residence inside the castle walls, the boy fell to his knees.

'Sire,' he said. 'As my poor mother lay dying, she bade me promise that I would not leave the cottage in which we had lived together until such time as I should find a bride who would be content to share it with me. In this way, said she, I will know that my bride's love for me is true.' The good king wept to hear the wisdom of the wise mother and went his way.

So it came to be that the young woodsman lived alone in his cottage in great contentment; the forest was his friend, neither wolf, nor bear, nor lynx held any terror for him. Only when the moon was full and the forest glade was filled with silver light, did the young boy know fear. He would bar the door, pull in the cord that lifted the latch, and lie with his woodsman's axe beside his bed. Then, while he listened to the sounds of the night about him, he would remember his mother's words.

'My son,' she had whispered, 'There is one secret that I must tell you now that you must pass on to no man, not even to the king himself. Come close, my love; my voice is failing.' The boy knelt and took the dying woman's hand. 'All is not well within the castle walls. Our king is just and our king is noble but you must know that there lives within the castle walls a monster over which he has no power. Once a month, at midnight, when the moon is full, this monster creeps forth from his lair and roams the castle at his will.'

'Mother dear,' cried the boy, trembling like a leaf. 'What could this monster want with me?' His poor mother drew him close.

'He seeks the flesh of one who is both young and fair,' she said, and here the poor woman wept and trembled in a way that the boy did not understand. He pressed a cup of water to her lips. 'Listen to me, son, for here the danger lies. The people of the castle are now too old for this foul monster's meat, but you, my son, though manly for your age, are both young and fair.' Terror alone held back the poor boy's tears.

'Mother, what must I do to save myself?' and he bent to hear her whispered words.

'Watch the waxing moon, my son, do not forget! On the night that it rises full, pull in the cord and bar the door. Open it to no one, fair or foul. Beware of honeyed words!' At this the woman lay back in the boy's arms and died.

A twelve-month passed; at each full moon the boy pulled in the cord, and barred the door. He lay trembling, waiting for the monster's stealthy tread, but all he heard were the sounds of the forest. In the mornings that followed the full moon he would say to himself. 'Surely, in her last hours, my dear mother

was wandering in her mind; there is no monster.' On the thir-
teenth month that followed his mother's death, the moon was
late to rise and so the boy forgot to bar the door. At midnight
he was woken by an unfamiliar step outside. A late traveller on
the forest road, perhaps? He sat up. His room was flooded with
silver light, and there was the moon standing full over the
castle roofs! The door – it was unbarred! Even as he leapt from
his bed he could see the cord tightening on the latch. Wielding
his axe, he struck at the cord. A cry of rage and pain met his
blow. He leapt to the window and there his terrified eyes
beheld the monster: grotesque and hunched, half human, half
animal. In a second it was gone, scrabbling and snarling
towards the castle walls. In the morning the boy saw that his
axe had passed clean through the door. Black blood speckled
the forest leaves.

It was a twelve-month before the monster came again but
this time it found the cord pulled in and the door barred
against it. Now, for the first time, it spoke and the boy sat up in
bed, wondering that a fiend so foul could fashion human
words. At one moment it was the voice of reason and concern.
Next it commanded, as if of royal right, then it was a voice of
silk. But when it took on the sweetness of honey the boy
remembered his mother's warning and pulled the blankets
over his head and listened no more. From this time on, scarcely
a month passed without a visit from the fiend but still the boy
kept the door barred against him. Then one day everything
changed.

It had come about that, since the moon last waned, a lady of
grace and nobility had come to live within the castle walls, and
with her came her daughter, a maid of just thirteen years,
lovely as any princess. To all within the castle, she shone like a
ray of sunshine. Her laughter echoed down the corridors, and
the sound of her feet running from room to room made even
the old feel young again. Within days she had so filled the
thoughts of the young forester that he was sure that he would

burst for joy. When the full moon came, and he barred the door, he looked forward to a night of thinking of the maid. He was thus engaged when the monster spoke:

'So, boy, we have a visitor within the castle walls?' The monster's tones were warm and honeyed, but the boy did not think before he answered.

'Oh yes, her laughter is like the ringing of bells, and the patter of her feet is like the sound of running water ...'

'Go on, my boy...?'

The boy laughed, 'What joy at last to have someone in the castle who is both young and fair ...' Even as he spoke, his blood ran cold. His mother's words were sharp in his ears: *He seeks the flesh of one both young and fair.* What had he said? How had he not thought? In vain he tried to undo his words. 'Her beauty is nothing to speak of, and ... and she is older than she looks ...' When the monster spoke again, the honeyed tones were gone.

'Do you think I do not know? Do you think I have not feasted my eyes on her, too? Why should I waste my time rattling at your barred door when I doubt not that hers hangs merely on the latch? Surely she will be sweeter meat than you!'

'Stop!' cried the boy. 'You must not touch her!'

'And how will you stop me, safe in your snug little home?'

'Take me instead, but spare the girl!' And the boy thought of his promise to his mother and wept.

'Perhaps you are over-tough by now?'

'Do with me what you will, but promise me to spare the maid.'

'Open the door and I promise that the girl will be spared at least until the next full moon.'

In terror and despair the boy opened the door. The monster's teeth were like daggers, and his eyes were like burning coals, and over all his parts clung a coating of green slime. The boy fell back. 'Give me your right arm,' the fiend commanded. The boy held it out, whereupon the foul creature seized it and bit it off at the shoulder. Then he set about eating it, drooling most horribly the while.

'How will I be able to cut wood in the forest now?' lamented the boy.

'Your arm will have grown again by the morning,' said the monster between mouthfuls. 'But remember, from now on, your right arm is mine, my mark will be on it and no matter how much you wash you will never be able to wash it clean.' Having finished his meal, the creature prepared to depart. 'Remember, boy, if I find your door closed against me again I will not knock but will go to seek a fairer feast.'

Jacquot stopped his reading. The pale light of the candle lit his face; a dew of sweat hazed his forehead.

'Go on,' Louise willed, 'how does it end?' Her eyes followed his down to the place where his finger still lingered. From that point on the page was blank. Perhaps he didn't know how to end it? Then, like a stab between the eyes, she realised why he had stopped. Hadn't M. Morteau warned that the local people would often hide real happenings within their folk tales? This tale of Jacquot's was about some real experience. The boy had not ended it for the simple reason that the tale had not run its course. A chill of real horror ran down her back. He didn't know what the ending was because the monster would come again!

To begin with, all Louise could do was to extend to Jacquot a wordless aura of sympathy and understanding. When he was sufficiently recovered, she began to talk, as she had talked to Pierre, in a silent flow of words, until in the end he responded, and the flow became an exchange. Jacquot leant against the mantelpiece, his head on his arms, while Louise probed gently, testing doors that even his gruesome story had failed to open. When, however, she asked, 'What does he do to you?' and he responded, it was her own mind that closed in self protection.

'Who is he, Jacquot?'

'A monster!' He said vehemently, 'but he's been like a father to me.' He gathered up his implements and his book and was gone. Louise was left dumbfounded.

All through the following days and nights Louise teased at the problem. There was no doubt in her mind that Jacquot was the boy in the story, and that Marie was certainly the 'young and fair' maiden. But who was this monster who had been 'like a father' to Jacquot? Who could command him 'as if of royal right' and leave him reluctant to utter his name. Then gradually she realised that she did know, and that she too had been reluctant to form his name. Dear God, how long had Jacquot been paying some dreadful price for Marie's safety?

'Jacquot,' she said without preamble, when he came the following week. 'The moon was new last week, so next week it will be full. You must finish your story before the next full moon. If you write what I tell you, I think we can stop this "monster" once and for all.'

'But what about Marie?' he asked.

'Marie will be safe. The "monster", as you call him, will come to me, not to her.'

'But how? I can't let you …'

'Of course you can. What harm can he do to a picture?' Louise was less confident than she sounded but pressed on relentlessly. 'You have a good memory?' The boy nodded. 'Well listen to me …' She told him what she thought he should say, drawing on the example of Gaston's bravery as he faced down the conspirators in this very chateau. As she went on she felt him engaging with her, nodding and then even making suggestions of his own. When he left her he seemed to be a different boy. She, on the other hand, wondered what she had done!

CHAPTER 17

The Rainbow Bridge

As he set out for the woodcutter's hut, the Count reminded himself, as he always did on these occasions, how good he had been to Jacquot. He had arranged that the boy had an education far above his station as a woodcutter; he had seen him clothed and fed in the chateau kitchens. The boy owed him. Surely it was a small price to ask for a little pleasure in return? He even felt justified in what he was about to do; in fact it was an act of love, he argued.

He stepped silently across the cobbles of the yard, feeling the familiar euphoria that elevated him to some awful height between the chateau and the moon. It was as though he were a tightrope walker. For him, love was a balance between desire and fear that his own desire might consume him.

He was surprised, and a little pleased, to see that the boy had lit a lamp; there was a yellow glow in his window, homely in the steel bright glare of the moon.

'Jacquot, it is I,' he called, trying to keep the hunger from his voice. In one sudden movement the door was snatched open and there stood Jacquot, a gleaming axe cradled on his arm. Lord, how the boy had grown, the Count thought in surprise, but it was the axe that held his gaze, the head had been polished till it shone … if the boy had polished the head, what had he done to the blade? Jacquot raised the axe an inch. What was this? The boy wasn't supposed to behave like this; he had always been submissive before. The Count's mouth had gone dry. Despite himself, he took a step backwards, and in doing so betrayed his cowardice to both Jacquot and himself. Rank and position meant nothing when standing alone in the face of cold steel. His legs felt weak and his hunger of a moment before turned to the nausea of fear.

'All right, Jacquot, all right. Not tonight then?' He was horrified to hear himself gibbering. 'What ... what do you want?'

'Monsieur le Comte, you are to read this.' To his amazement, the boy thrust a sheaf of paper at him. He took it. 'Now Monsieur, if you please, turn about. *En avant, marchez!*'

'You can't order ...'

'I can and I will. Now, walk towards the kitchen, and remember, I am one step behind you.'

Jacquot stood over the Count while he lit a kitchen candle from the tiny wick that was left floating in oil so that the chateau would never be without a flame. The Count sat at the table and pressed down hard on the pages to prevent his hand from shaking.

'Now, read!' Jacquot commanded. He waited until the Count had scanned the first page, and then he stepped back.

'Where are you going?'

'I am going to stand watch outside Marie's door. I will not leave her unprotected.' The Count winced, but he turned the page and read on.

It had been Louise's idea that Jacquot should guard Marie, not so much because she thought the girl would be in

danger, but to get Jacquot away from the man who had
dominated him for so much of his life. But if she could have
seen the young hero now, she would have had no reason to
fear, indeed she might have wished for his protection
herself.

The Count's hands closed convulsively on the final pages of
Jacquot's story, crumpling them cruelly. How dare he? Who
did that little ingrate think he was? An image of Jacquot
barring the door to the hut with the polished axe flashed
across his mind and he groaned as he remembered his own
cowardice. He knew who was responsible for all of this –
that girl in the picture. She had bewitched him, as he had
known she would from the moment Gaston had presented
the picture to him. How many times had he stood in front of
her at night, holding his candle high, fascinated and drawn
by that face? He had never experienced such a feeling
before, a longing to know her that rose from deep in his
heart's core. He was used to having his way, but that girl
held him at a distance, challenging him, questioning him
until he would have to leave the room, in case she walked
out of the canvas and he would have to answer for himself.
Now he would have to destroy her.

He thought back to Celine, Jacquot's mother. He had
loved her, at first with delight, and then with a passion that
had bordered on insanity. When the boy was born, he could
have taken her in to be his mistress … his wife even. God
knew there were enough examples of such behaviour in his
family, but by that stage genuine love and compassion were
no longer enough for him. The heights of passion that he
craved could only be satisfied by the thrill of his night time

forays and the rush of power that came with total control over his victims. To begin with, he persuaded himself that the moon genuinely did have a role in commanding his passions; that it was not really he who prowled the corridors and forest glades, but someone else over whom he had no control, and for whom he had no responsibility. But then he began to enjoy the suffering he was causing to his victims and claimed it for himself. The moon became a mechanism to foster and curb his passions in turn. The people of the chateau began to re-tell their old stories of predatory monsters who hunted by the full moon. Of course he spoke out against such tales, dismissing them as peasant superstition, but secretly he was pleased; the danger of discovery fed his appetite further.

But where had this appetite sprung from? Where had it all started, and why did it seem to be his destiny to destroy the things he loved?

Up until the day of his fourth birthday, little Auguste du Bois thought he could do no wrong; whatever he wished for was his. Now he couldn't remember the cause of his punishment on that day, but it had come in the form of a slap on the hand from his mother, who, until that moment, had been the source of all the love in his life. With the smack came the command to go out into the garden and not come back until he had found his manners. Tears had given way to resentment, and then to the absolute conviction that Mama no longer loved him. He wandered about the ragged edge of the garden, nurturing this feeling. Butterflies clustered on the purple flowers of the knapweed. Most of these were 'forest browns' that lived along the edge of the trees, and therefore familiar. All at once a butterfly that had had its wings folded spread them wide, and a flash of gorgeous colour caused the boy to stop in his tracks. On the lower wings were two jewelled eyes that appeared to be looking at him. The upper wings rose like two surprised eyebrows above them. Never had he seen anything so beautiful. He knelt down slowly, careful not to disturb it. The peacock eyes returned his gaze. Closer and closer the boy moved until he was within inches of the butterfly. It seemed to fill his whole view; every antenna, every scale, every hair was perfect, while in the background the meadow grasses became a green fuzz into which the knapweed bled in soft purple smudges. The symmetry, the unexpected colours, the fragility and the fact that the eyes returned his look so fearlessly, enraptured him. He was held fast by those eyes; they promised a love that would replace the vacuum left by his mother's rejection.

At that moment the butterfly closed its wings, like a book snapped shut in mid-sentence, and the eyes disappeared. Sudden fury welled up inside the boy; the eyes had no right to disappear. They had betrayed him, like his mother. But he could deal with this betrayal; this fluttery creature was smaller than him, weaker than him. The smack he dealt it with his chubby hand was a very good imitation of his mother's slap of half an hour ago. He sat back on his haunches and looked at the fragments of his passion of a moment ago. He felt regret, but also satisfaction. It was the first time he had tasted power, and he liked it.

As he walked back towards the chateau, his feeling of power grew and grew. He was a giantkiller. What did he care about smacked hands and Judas kisses when he had found the ultimate solution for those weaker than him?

His mother looked up from her sewing as he passed. 'And where did you get that smug little smile from, Auguste?' she asked, not unkindly.

The Count sat staring into space, the pages of Jacquot's story rucked up under his hands. So, it was: 'a princess, with hair the colour of sunlight, and a dress of emerald green' that had given the boy the sword to slay the monster. The Count ground his teeth; he could feel the pulse beginning to throb in his temples. Anger was replacing humiliation. There was still time to retrieve something of the night. He would deal with the boy tomorrow, but now his focus was that picture. He would show them all who had the real power around here.

Some part of his rational mind argued that a picture was just a picture: canvas, paint and a wooden stretcher. But he knew that it was more than that; this *was* witchcraft – as Gaston had known full well. And the cure for witchcraft was fire.

The Count's anger was so intense that Louise felt its energy long before he came into the room. For the first time she felt that her existence was in real danger. This wasn't like Colette's petulant flick with the duster or Gaston's threat to ride through her when she was forcing him to help the peasant and his cart. With a conscious effort of will, she moved from her picture to the opposite side of the room. At that moment the door was thrown open and the Count du Bois burst in.

He strode down the room to where Louise's portrait hung, protecting the flickering flame of his candle with one hand. He swung to face the picture. 'Witch!' he screamed. 'I should never have let you into the chateau. Bloody Gaston planted you here to spy on me. I could see it in your face the moment I laid eyes on you. And now the boy defies me. Damn it! My own– ' she heard him check himself. He held up Jacquot's crumpled manuscript and waved it at the portrait. 'Le Jacquot, my log boy,' he said scornfully, 'he fancies himself as the new Charles Perrault! This is my reward for giving him the education of a gentleman! He has the cheek to lecture me.

'*A princess in a green dress!*' he went on sarcastically, his voice rising: 'Is it just chance that you have a green dress? Like hell it is! All I ask is his indulgence on this one night in the month, and he defies me, and gives me this to read. Do I look like a monster?' Suddenly a catch came into the Count's voice and his anger seemed to fade. 'And what about you … Louise? You bewitched Gaston, didn't you? And he had to get rid of you.' He put the candle down on one side of the wide grate; then he reached up and began to lift Louise's portrait from its hook. 'I am truly sorry for what I am about to do, but you will have to go. If Jacquot had lit the fire tonight this would have been easy.'

At last Louise understood. He was about to destroy her portrait. Fool that she was, she'd thought only of physical danger to herself. Her portrait gone – it was unthinkable! The whole of the last summer of her short life flashed through her mind. Pieter had prepared that very canvas before they had even met. She thought of how, at the Master's bidding, her face had emerged from the canvas, brush stroke after tiny brush stroke. She thought of Pieter's pride at his work on the Turkey carpet, and of the Master's promise that one day she might live again in the minds of others. And now it would all be destroyed: their legacy, her very existence. The Count was leaning forward into the cavern-ous fireplace, holding her picture in its heavy frame, like an inquisitor preparing a heretic for death at the stake. The pyre was ready, all he had to do was to reach out for the candle and the picture would be in flames. And Louise could stand it no more.

'No! Not my picture!' she screamed.

The cry pierced the Count like an arrow. He started, lost his grip on the picture and let it fall. A single slender splinter rose from the setting of logs and burst through the canvas at the very point where Louise's ankle emerged from her dress. He saw the tear and winced as if feeling her pain himself. Where had that scream come from? He lurched to his feet and turned, and there she was, arms outstretched, appealing to him.

It was the Count imagining the agony in her ankle that transferred the pain to Louise. She gave a gasp, stumbled on the hem of her skirt, and fell to the ground, the silk of her dress spreading about her like a butterfly's wings. She heard the Count's coarse shout, and knew that she had woken the monster in him, but she was still trapped in the folds of her dress. He was coming at her now, around the end of the long dining room table, tearing at his cravat. She had no doubts about his intentions. She freed herself and was in the very act of rising when suddenly he stopped, his hands palms-out to her.

'Don't move,' he whispered hoarsely. Later Louise would realise that, by some chance of light or posture, she had cap-tured the precise pose that the Master had caught when he painted her portrait. The moonlight spilled across her face in the same way as the light had fallen on her in the studio. She froze, maintaining the position, as she had done for so many hours for the Master in Delft. Gradually the Count sank to his knees, then his head dropped, and he began to weep behind the protection of his hands. Long, silent convulsions shook his frame. Louise dared not move. Finally he looked up, and he began to wipe his face with his loosened cravat.

'I'm sorry!' he said, and this time it sounded genuine.

Louise attempted to straighten up, but found her muscles stiff and sore. Without thinking, she stretched her hand out and the Count took it and raised her to her feet. Suddenly he dropped her hand, as though it were a red-hot coal.

'But you are flesh and blood,' he said in wonder, looking at his own hand.' I ... I could have done anything to you!'

'And had every intention of doing so, I believe.' Louise moved away, putting the width of the table between them.

While the full moon sank behind the trees and the first grey of dawn lit the veil of mist that hung over the meadow outside, Louise questioned the Count about his past. She dragged him back, from his present abuse of Jacquot, to the deflowering of Jacquot 's mother, a mere child at the time. When Celine became pregnant, there was the betrayal of his promises of marriage and protection. Gradually the Count began to pour out the whole story. Whenever he tried to cover himself with excuses or with a false cloak of decency, Louise shredded them with ruthless efficiency. And when he tried to find refuge in his childhood injustice she pointed out that he had had forty years to put this right. While she spoke she felt that Annie, her old Calvinistic nurse, was at her side, not letting her waver even an inch. There was no redemption for evil done; this man was damned, and she let him know it.

'And now what will happen? Will you wait till the next full moon and start again?' she demanded.

'No, I cannot,' he said.

Louise looked at him in surprise. It wasn't the answer she'd expected. She'd been anticipating more false promises. 'You always have in the past,' she pointed out.

'Until this evening, Mademoiselle Louise, I would have said that whatever attack you could make on my moral behaviour, at least my courage was intact. You see, I firmly believed that it took courage for me to walk about the chateau and the forest paths at night. I thought it took courage to spread terror and to force my will upon the helpless.' The Count paused, then shrugged. 'You could call that my last illusion. Tonight Jacquot confronted me with an axe. It is the first time that one of my victims has put me in physical danger and I knew fear for the first time in my life. My legs turned to jelly. I am a coward, Mademoiselle Eeden; when you damn me, you can add that to your condemnation.'

'Oh no! It is not me that damns you, nor God either. But the years, hours, minutes of suffering you have caused – nothing more, nothing less. You had forty years to bring happiness to the world; those years are irredeemably lost: that is damnation.'

She had said what had to be said. Suddenly Louise was overcome by a physical tiredness that she had hardly known since she had been a living person in Delft. She put her head on her arms and went to sleep leaning on the dining room table.

Jacquot gripped the handle of his axe and pressed his back against Marie's door. It was still dark, but a bell had rung somewhere down the corridor. There were sounds of movement below: a door banged, someone shouted. He wanted to rush down. What was going on? Could Mademoiselle Louise be in danger? But he couldn't abandon Marie. A light was approaching along the corridor, accompanied by rapid steps. It was Marie's mother; she was fully dressed. She stopped in her tracks when she saw him.

'What on earth are you doing here, Jacquot?'

'I'm guarding Marie, Madame. There were st ... strange happenings. I was afraid for her.'

'Oh, you are silly! It's only the Count getting ready to travel.'

'He's going away?' Jacquot asked incredulously, 'In the middle of the night?'

'Yes. Apparently he's had his bags packed for weeks; there must be some special reason. Anyway, Marie's perfectly safe; you should go back to bed.' She hurried on.

As the housekeeper bustled away she thought of Jacquot. He was such a nice lad, and Marie liked him. What a pity he had no prospects.

Downstairs she found organised chaos. The Count was trying to hammer simple instructions into heads still fogged with sleep. The coachman was snatching a hasty breakfast at the kitchen table; God knew when he would get his next meal. When she asked him where they were bound he shrugged his shoulders without stopping chewing. Gradually the turmoil died down, the bags were stowed; everyone waited while the Count busied himself with some last minute business in the dining hall. A first glimmer of sun was breaking through the branches of the trees.

Louise was woken by two loud thumps on the window. She looked up and was surprised to see sunlight.

'What was that?' she asked.

The Count, who was sorting through papers at the other end of the table, said: 'I suspect some small bird being chased by a hawk mistook the window for the sky. It happens sometimes. The hawk usually comes off the worst.'

'That's sad,' Louise said.

The Count turned to look at her. 'So you really are there. I thought perhaps I had only dreamed about you.'

'And thrown my picture into the fireplace in your sleep?' Louise said bitterly. She noticed the pile of papers. 'What are you doing?'

'Settling my affairs. I'm going away... to England. Half the aristocracy of France has already gone.'

'Will you come back?'

'Probably not.'

'And your estate ... the chateau?' she asked. He looked up at her, his face older, lines of defeat and resignation etched around his mouth. And there was something else – a sort of peace as though he was in some way relieved at having told it all.

'Should I leave it to the boy?' he asked.

'Jacquot? Does he know you are his father?'

'No,' the Count said.

'Then don't tell him. You have forfeited a father's rights. Leaving him the chateau will just involve unwanted explanations. Let the boy leave his monsters behind him. All he needs is security and a future worthy of his talents. If you have a small property, leave him that, and enough income to marry young Marie ... or the girl of his choice. He will be able to accept that as some kind of apology for what you have done to him.'

'There is a dower house, I will leave him that; it's a pretty place. I'll do that for you.'

'Not for *me*, do it for Jacquot's mother! Dear God, I hope you treated her better than you did your son! I have another request. You still hold some acres in Les Clos du Bois – leave these to Gaston; he saved your head.'

'I'm not sure now that he did me a favour. All right, Gaston will have it all.'

'Have you heard anything of him recently?'

'His father told me that he was headed for Italy, adjutant to a General Bonaparte, I think.'

The Count drew up the necessary papers with care. He went out to get Marie's mother to witness his signature. When he came back Louise was fading, partly out of weariness, but partly because she no longer held the Count's interest. She made one last effort to impose her will on him.

'Monsieur le Comte, whatever your reasons for being the man you are, never forget the damage you have caused to those you profess to love. Go from here now. Leave Jacquot to try to recover from the wounds you have inflicted, and never again pollute love with perversion.'

The people of the chateau moved in a daze, going about their chores, but wondering why they were still doing them. The Count had gone that morning, yet they kept to their orbits, still circling about the point where he had been.

Jacquot came to light the fire in the banqueting hall. It was dark in the recess of the fireplace so he put down his bucket of coals and turned to begin rekindling the fire. He gasped when he saw Louise's picture lying askew on top of the logs, a ragged splinter emerging through the torn canvas. He gave a small cry of sympathy, and then he leant forward and carefully eased the canvas off the spike. He stood back, holding the painting, at a loss to know what to do. The blank space on the wall was the obvious place for the picture, but he couldn't just put it back, not with that tear. It would be like leaving her to bleed to death. He found the baize cloth they used when visitors came to play cards, wrapped the picture in it, and hurried down the corridor towards the back entrance.

He hesitated at the door of the kitchen; he would have to pass through, and Marie was there. He glanced in. The girl was totally absorbed, trying to feed chopped-up worms to a wounded bird she had rescued from outside the banqueting hall. Jacquot slipped through silently and went out to his cottage. He slid the picture under his bed, and with a murmur of apology, hurried back to his hot coals. When the fire was lit he returned to the kitchen and lingered there for a while. Marie was cross, and looking a little green. She didn't like handling worms and the ungrateful bird wouldn't eat. When Jacquot pointed out that goldfinches didn't eat worms, she wasn't sure whether to be embarrassed or relieved. She cheered up at once though when Jacquot said that it might sing for her, so she sent him out to find some spilled grain from the stables.

Jacquot immersed himself in the task of repairing Louise's canvas. He went about it with extraordinary thoroughness. His first job, which proved the most difficult, was to pull the two sides of the tear together. After several failures he found that if he wetted threads of new linen, which he teased from dressmaking remnants that he had begged from Marie, he could stick these to the back of the canvas. As the linen shrank it pulled the sides of the tear together. Sticking the threads down was a problem until he learned from a local carpenter how to make glue by boiling animal hooves. He did this in the kitchen until Marie's mother complained about the smell. He told no one about the picture, working on it at night, pulling in the latch cord and working by the light of two candles to avoid shadows. Little by little the tear closed, until it was hardly visible on the surface.

Jacquot talked while he worked, rather as a groom will talk to a horse in a soothing patter. He avoided turning the portrait over, other than to review the progress of his repair. Something strange and wonderful, but also a bit frightening, had happened between him and the girl in the picture, and he was trying to shut his mind to that time. But he still felt the need to talk to her, so he reported that Marie's mother was now the official caretaker, and explained that the Commune was running the farm, but that not much work was being done. The chateau people presumed that the Count had taken the picture of the girl in the green dress with him when he left. Jacquot would, of course, return it when it was mended, but it was not ready yet. He made a crude box for the picture, which he could slide under his bed. This not only concealed it but also protected it from any possible further damage.

Knowing that her portrait was safe gave Louise the same feeling of security that she had felt when it was enclosed in the travelling box the boys had made for her in Holland. Ever since the picture had been damaged, she had become very conscious of how vulnerable it was. Though she liked M. Morteau's idea of her being an ambassador, she was also a guardian, with a duty to preserve Pieter and the Master's place in history. She would not willingly put the portrait at risk again.

The peace and quiet of Jacquot's hut was welcome after the turmoil of the Count's departure. And Louise did not feel alone; she hadn't been forgotten. Colette, Gaston and Pierre consciously and unconsciously thought of her, though Louise often had to use her imagination to interpret what she was seeing through their eyes.

Colette had been waiting for this moment. She and Jean Brouchard were like two pranksters as they looked out of the high windows of M. Morteau's office, waiting to see if their victim, M. Morteau, would take their bait. Up to now he had been steadfast in his refusal to have anything to do with the 'charlatans', as he called them, who had been given portions of the vineyard by the Count in order to win favour with the revolutionaries. It had not surprised him that they had been unable to make anything better than *vin ordinaire*, or even, in one case, vinegar, from those grapes. The man who was now approaching him was one of these 'charlatans', and he carried an offer, carefully worked out by Colette and M. Brouchard so as to be to the advantage of all. The proposal was that he would hand over the management of his acres to M. Morteau. In return, he would get an agreed number of bottles of superior vintage made from grapes from the whole vineyard. It had been Colette's suggestion that these bottles should have special labels, carrying not just the prestigious name 'Côtes du Bois', but the name of the new proprietor as well. The question now was whether Papa Morteau would accept the deal.

The two conspirators watched the introductory shaking of hands. They noticed M. Morteau stiffen as the man identified himself. Would he walk away? The miller was crushing poor Colette's arm in his anxiety. Now the two were talking tentatively ... now in earnest. M. Morteau was shrugging doubtfully but they were still talking, walking up and down.

'Go on, Papa ...' Colette urged, 'Look, he's interested.' The two men were pointing towards the now neglected plot. There it was! A nod from M. Morteau, his gestures were getting wider, more expansive. Now he had seized the visitor's elbow.

'They're off!' shouted M. Brouchard. Sure enough, there they went, Papa's arms moving like the sails of a windmill. Jean Brouchard seized Colette about the waist, waltzed her down the length of the office and the building shook.

Louise had been seeing the whole incident through Colette's eyes, when suddenly the room seemed to be turning round and round. It took her a moment to realise that they were dancing. Now she laughed with them in their triumph. What Colette was trying to do was clever and foresighted. Surely the other owners would also realise the advantages of having their wine made for them. When Gaston came home he would find that not only was the Count's personal vineyard his, but that his father had the management of the whole vineyard again.

That vision faded and Louise relaxed. It would be nice if she could pass the good news on to Gaston, but she knew that the very best she could do was to turn her mind towards him and hope that he would feel her happiness. It was, therefore, possibly no coincidence that she soon found herself seeing steep crags sloping down towards a sea as brilliantly blue as the lapis lazuli that Pieter had been grinding on the day she had first gone to the Master's studio. Gaston must be on the march again. As far ahead as she could see, an army of men was winding along a steep coast road, men clad in dusty blue and carrying muskets, their rations of bread pierced on their bayonets. Gaston must be following an upper path, 'guarding the flank,' as she had heard him say. The soldier in front turned, and she recognised Pierre, smiling and pointing. He looked sunburned and well.

'Yes, Italy!' she heard Gaston's voice. So, that blue sea must be the Mediterranean. Italy, she sighed enviously; a country set in lapis lazuli!

Jacquot's gentle ministrations eased not only the hurt in her foot, but the hurt to her heart as well. She liked the scents of the hut, and the feeling of the forest outside. The weather warmed, the door stood open most of the time, and she could listen to the rasp of his saw and the *clunk clunk* of his axe as he worked.

But gradually Louise recognised that there was something wrong. She could feel spring all around them but somehow it wasn't touching them. New shoots were sprouting everywhere, but the boy and she were not mending. Although the picture was almost whole again, Louise was not. It was as though the evil that had touched Jacquot had penetrated her soul as well. They were like a pair of sick vines, gradually dying back.

Her almost daily glimpses of life in the winery and of Gaston and Pierre in Italy only helped to feed her depression. She was more and more oppressed by her future. Was she always to be a captive of her sixteen years, never able to fulfil any relationship as time drew out the differences between herself and the people she learned to love? Would she always have to step aside for someone else? The rainbow that had bridged the gulf between herself and Pieter came back to torment her. Should she have abandoned reality and crossed the rainbow bridge to Pieter? But how could she leave Jacquot, who still needed her, and Gaston, Colette and the others who had recreated her in their minds? As she and Jacquot slipped deeper into a morass of depression the temptation to turn back in time grew stronger and stronger.

Jacquot's reaction to his malaise was to become a recluse. The more spring spoke to him, the stronger became his desire to be alone. His feelings of being unclean were getting worse, not better. When he was working outside in the forest, the air, the wind, the rain and the rough wood scoured his mind and kept him clean. But when he came close to people he became conscious of his contamination. In the kitchen he would sit as far away from everyone as he could, convinced that they would notice the smell of corruption from him. The customary morning handshake had become a torture; his own fairy tale came back to haunt him, and he half expected to see green slime on any hand he had just shaken.

It was young Marie who precipitated matters. Jacquot had come running into the hut, with Marie hot on his heels. There had been some exchange between them, and Louise was delighted to see them happy together. Jacquot had retreated to the end of the room. Marie advanced, arms akimbo, challenging him. Jacquot was trapped.

'Did I hear you shout: '*Où est la Marie?*' *La Marie?* As if I were a kitchen maid?' She was advancing step by step. Jacquot, half laughing, half nervous, was looking for a way past her. 'Log boy… I'm coming to get you!'

Without warning, it happened. Jacquot crumpled down against the wall, cowering. 'Get away,' he hissed. But Marie was enjoying her game.

'I'm coming for you ...'

'Get away.' It was almost a scream.

Suddenly Jacquot was on his feet, his face inflamed and his arms outstretched. Marie, frightened, screamed and ran from the hut. Jacquot made to follow and then stumbled and stopped, leaning aghast against the door.

'Come back, Marie' he called ... 'Please, I didn't mean it.'

Night came and he sat hunched on the edge of his bed, so far turned in on himself that Louise was afraid that she too might be drawn into his abyss. His voice seemed to have an echo when he spoke.

'I nearly grabbed her,' he said. 'I love her, but I wanted suddenly to crush her.' Then he whispered something that sent a shiver deep into Louise's core. 'Dear God,' he said, 'am I doomed to become like him?'

He dropped his head on to his knees and began to cry, a dry, heaving, tearless grief that Louise thought would break him apart. She talked to him then, as he had talked to her, about anything that came to mind, just so that he would know he wasn't alone. When she ran out of things to say she even found herself singing him a silly little Dutch nursery rhyme: *All the ducks are swimming on the water, fol de lol de li do ... fol de lol de li do.* It was then that he began crying properly.

The following day Jacquot was very downcast. When he came in, Louise didn't like to ask if he had made it up with Marie. As he moved about she heard him singing to himself as he used to do. This time however she recognised the song: *fol de lol de li do ...*

Then he asked: 'Mademoiselle, how is it that you know how I feel?'

'I don't, Jacquot. We each have our own feelings, but I saw the Count's lust too, you know, and although he did not hurt me, he desecrated my picture instead. You have been healing me by mending my picture, but it will never be the same.'

'Will I always be unclean then, contaminating anyone I touch?'

'I don't think we can undo something that is done, Jacquot, but we can change our understanding of it. When I am unhappy I have a dream in which I see a rainbow, and I long to cross the rainbow and go back to what might have been, to go back to Pieter, the boy I loved. But yet I hear my father's voice, saying: "Think about it, Louise. Is that really what your rainbow means? Think of the science of it".'

Jacquot looked into the distance for a moment. 'I have a dream too,' he said. 'Ever since he first came to me. In my dream I am in a forest glade ... there is a cliff, a flat shelf of rock, from which a waterfall plunges into a pool of the purest water. I just know that if I can stand under that waterfall it will wash me clean. But he ... he is always there, laughing, dodging about and blocking my way.'

'But he's gone now, Jacquot. There's no one to hold you back. You must dream that dream again.'

'But what about you?'

'You can take me too.'

'How can I take a picture under the waterfall?'

'I can be as real as you make me, Jacquot. Please take me there.'

They walked together in Jacquot's dream.

'We'll soon be there,' he said, taking courage from her company. Louise enjoyed being with him. She remembered how she had looked out over the fields from the walls of Delft with Pieter and had seen the familiar countryside with his artist's eye. Now she was experiencing this French forest as Jacquot did. His was a world of smells and small sounds; the swish of their feet through the leaves changed as they passed under oak, or beech, or Spanish chestnut. When something struck the ground near them he made her stand still till the thrower, a red squirrel, peeked out to see if his nut had found its mark. He got her to listen, her ear to the trunk of an ancient tree, to the click of beetles feasting under the bark. He got her to fill her head with the heady smell of resin where a lone pine grew on a stony bluff. After a while the trees began to thin and a stream joined them, hurrying past, chattering to itself about some recent adventure. Louise could feel Jacquot's apprehension mounting.

'It's here that he stops me, where I can see the waterfall.' Jacquot whispered. 'I'm afraid ...'

'Don't be, Jacquot. I told you, he's gone.'

'Look,' he said, pointing through the trees. There it was, a rocky escarpment notched at the skyline where a single sheet of water sprang from its lip before arching down to plunge into a pool below. They stepped forward and the trees seemed to draw back as if making way for them.

The boy still hesitated. 'Go on, don't be shy,' Louise encouraged. He stepped forward, warily, like a child, check-ing for lurking monsters, wondering if this enchantment was really for him.

'Will you come too?'

'No,' Louise said. 'This is your dream, your place.' She

looked the other way as he stripped, but turned to watch as he stepped into the water, lifting his feet delicately like a fawn. When he reached the cascade he stepped forward, holding his hands above his head to break the flow. The water burst over him, spreading a fine spray into the low sunlight, and a rainbow appeared, arching over and around him. It was as if he was holding it above his head in his hands. Then he spread his arms so that the water thundered on to his head and shoulders. She had seen a drawing of a figure like this somewhere – in the Master's studio maybe – a symbol of mankind, enclosed in a circle. But here the circle was a rainbow, and Jacquot walked through it into the space behind the curtain of water where she could see him scrubbing himself from head to toe.

Louise went to the edge of the pool and dipped her hands into the clear water. She washed her face and drank a little from her cupped hands, and felt refreshed. She was tempted to follow Jacquot under the waterfall, but this was his future, not hers, and it was time for her to go. But he had given her the sign she had been looking for. There was no magical way back to Pieter; the gulf of time separated them. The rainbow was an invitation to go forward, to whatever the future had in store.

Louise left Jacquot to his dream. She never knew where it took him, but if she had heard that, on his waking, the goldfinch in Marie's room had put back its head and sung for joy, she might have guessed.

CHAPTER 18

The Army of Italy

In March 1796, when the Hussars of Auxerre, including Gaston's troop, had ridden down into the city of Nice to join Bonaparte's starved and ragged 'army of Italy', they looked like strutting pheasants in a yard full of moulting hens. That evening Bonaparte addressed the rabble army: *Soldiers, you are naked, badly fed ... Rich provinces and great towns will be in your power, and in them you will find honour, glory, wealth. Soldiers of Italy, will you be wanting in courage and steadfastness?* Whatever about 'honour and glory', the word 'wealth' spoke to the dispirited men. Overnight the mood and appearance of the army changed. Rags were washed clean and muskets oiled. When the General inspected the newly arrived hussars and told them that it was their courage he wanted, not their whiskers, they caught the mood of the moment and cheered. Gaston sat motionless in his saddle during the inspection, staring straight ahead, as if carved out of wood. Bonaparte would never recognise him out of a whole brigade. However, when he came to Gaston he looked up. His Corsican accent was as rough as ever.

'Lieutenant Morteau, you will report to my headquarters this evening at five o'clock.'

Gaston was too astonished to do more than say, 'Monsieur le Général,' as he continued to stare straight ahead.

That evening he received orders to join the General

Bonaparte's entourage. As he was too junior to be a staff officer, he was appointed as a special courier. Having explained his orders, the General was about to turn away when Gaston dared to say:

'Mon Général, I have a request.' A flicker of disapproval crossed Bonaparte's face, but Gaston went on. 'I have a cadet, a superb horseman, I would like him to ride with me.'

'Why?'

'If one of us is wounded, the other will see that your orders get through.'

In the months that followed, the General's two couriers became known up and down the still hungry and ragged column that tramped down the coast back into Italy, to where Austria and her allies waited to confront them.

Now that spring had come, not only to the forest but also to the two occupants of the hut, Louise was able to enjoy the not infrequent glimpses of life with the army in Italy. Gaston was almost as bad at remembering her as he was about writing letters to Colette. When he did, it was at times of scenic beauty or relaxation. She would suddenly see Pierre across the flicker of a campfire, or hear him called to sing one of the songs of Normandy as the wine was passed around. Pierre was more constant. He had not been part of the pact to think of Louise, but he thought of her because thinking of her made him happy – sometimes in moments of elation, but also in times of stress, when even the hardened soldier's hand will steal to some hidden talisman or charm.

Though Louise had no way of reckoning time other than by following the season's changes, it was in fact 10th May 1796 when her reverie was broken by the sound of guns.

Smoke swirled across her vision and she realised that she was in Italy again. Ahead of her a horse and rider climbed up the side of a small knoll. Guns poked over a parapet of fresh earth. She could see a river glinting below. As the rider dismounted and handed his reins to a soldier he half turned; it was Gaston. So, Pierre was her eyes this time. She watched Gaston approach one of the guns where a smallish man was crouched over its sleek barrel. Soldiers with spikes and mallets were turning and elevating the gun following his directions. Now the man stood to one side, mouthed an order, and a soldier who had been standing by with a smouldering match stepped forward. He touched the burning tip to the powder in the touch-hole. A small flame spurted out and with an angry roar the gun leapt back – flame, then smoke, spouting from its muzzle. Pierre's horse must have shied, as Louise could see its head rise as the smoke swept past them. The man who had been sighting the gun was peering to see where his shot had landed. Suddenly everyone was cheering and the man smiled, slapped one hand on the other with satisfaction, and turned to Gaston; it was General Bonaparte himself! Gaston bent to shout in his ear and pointed up the river. The news must be good; the General nodded. Gaston stepped back and saluted. Then he looked up at Pierre and smiled. Louise's heart gave a great lurch, it was as if he was smiling at her.

All of the new landowners had taken up the winery's offer to work their vineyards for them. When Colette came out and stood watching M. Morteau give the orders of the day, Louise could see that the yard was full of men. 'Like the old days,' M. Morteau said, adding, 'If only we had Gaston back.'

The war in Italy seemed to be going on forever. When the grape harvest came, Louise could feel that Colette was missing Gaston just as she was. When she could summon the energy, she would try hard to convey to Colette that Gaston was all right. He was better about writing now, but letters still took many weeks to reach home.

Though she tried to be optimistic, Louise was far from happy. Pierre, clinging to his image of her for comfort and reassurance, was showing her far more of the horrors of war than she wanted to see, although it would never have occurred to him that he was doing this. Battles became names: Mantua, Lonato, Castiglione, Bassano, Arcola … It was at Lodi that the men started calling Bonaparte 'our little corporal,' because he had done a corporal's job by sighting the guns himself before the attack.

Then one day her whole vision was taken up with bodies, mostly clad in the blue of France, many of them intertwined with the grey uniforms of Austria. Pierre was searching among the fallen, looking for the bright colours of a hussar. Louise could hear the whimper in his breath and her own throat constricted in pain. Gaston must be missing! For half an hour they searched. Then the flap parted on a crudely erected tent and a man emerged. It was Gaston, his head newly bandaged. He turned at Pierre's shout and the image faded as Pierre forgot all about Louise in a joyful rush to his lieutenant.

Christmas passed but there was little festive fare for the French soldiers and even less for the starving Austrians besieged in the town of Mantua. Battle raged about Rivoli as the Austrian army from the north strove to relieve the siege and drive the French out of Italy.

Louise knew nothing about the reasons for the battle she was seeing through Pierre's eyes, but she could sense from his apprehension that disaster was imminent. She watched as the French line bent, held, then yielded. Now she could see Gaston thrusting orders into his tunic.

'The orders are for Lasalle to charge! Follow me, Pierre … but not too close.' Up the wide gorge they rode, the roar of battle behind them. Louise heard the whirring whine of a cannon ball, and the last clear vision she would remember from that day was seeing the track of the ball – a linear disturbance of the light – streaking inexorably towards the point where Gaston was riding ahead.

Pierre's appeal for help came so imperiously that Louise had no choice but to respond. Afterwards she remembered nothing. When the energy of the crisis was expended she was completely drained and had no idea what had happened to her during those dreadful minutes, or were they hours?

It took young Jacquot, working on her foot and chatting about the day's events, to restore her to the point at which she could remember even that something dreadful had happened. She put out a silent appeal to her soldiers in Italy. All she received in return was a picture of a two-storey house, a red tiled roof, with four small windows above and below, and for no good reason, a conviction that Gaston was still alive.

After their shared dream, Louise never appeared to Jacquot again. She had done for him what she could, and he seemed to accept that life was now of his own making. But when he talked to himself in his hut he liked to think that Louise was listening, so he included all the news that he thought might interest her. It was now 1798, and word had come of the success of the Italian campaign. Though Louise's conviction that Gaston was still alive never faltered, neither he nor Pierre sent her any more clear messages. Marie now spent more time in Jacquot's hut than she did in the chateau, but she made him keep his distance; she was not going to be any fallen lady. The political climate changed, and the Count's affairs were put in order. To his amazement, Jacquot found himself the owner of the pretty little dower house that stood apart from the chateau, and the possessor of a position of responsibility on the estate.

Quite suddenly, after an anxious wait of months, Louise began to get messages from Colette and Gaston again. Later she would learn that news of Gaston's wound had far outstripped news that he had survived. In her anxiety, poor Colette was too turned in on herself to share this with Louise. She could not work out how she knew, but it came as no surprise to Louise to hear that Gaston had lost a leg. Now, to her delight, Colette was showing her Gaston again, first on crutches, and then trying to walk with a wooden leg, assisted by Pierre. She had been worried about Pierre too, and was delighted to see him, but why was he not sending her his own images? She really missed this when Colette and Gaston were married. Colette had shared all the preparations with Louise, but on the day itself they both had other things to think of, so Pierre's view would have made all the difference.

It was through Jacquot that Louise heard the news that

there were to be visitors to the chateau: Captain Morteau from the winery, who had lost a leg in Italy, and his new wife, were expected. Also some poor lad who had served with the Captain in the wars.

Louise felt their presence as soon as their hired carriage passed Jacquot's hut on its way into the yard. Soon their pull on her was so strong that she let go and found herself back in the dining hall where her picture had hung. She stood just inside the curtains so that she could see them before they saw her. How they had changed! A white scar stood out on Gaston's forehead and his cork leg thumped on the polished floor as he walked. She wanted to rush and embrace him, but Colette was holding his arm, supporting him. For a long moment Gaston stared at the spot by the fireplace, and Louise could see images of herself flash through his mind.

'You'd have thought the scoundrel would have left her picture behind,' Gaston said to Colette. 'I suppose he thought it paid for the land, but I doubt that he will ever know her as we have. You know, I can almost feel her here. Dear Louise, if only she'd appear again now.'

Louise was just about to step out when she saw Pierre. He had drifted into the room after the others and was looking vacantly about him. Louise caught her breath; here was someone in real need. What had happened to him? Where was the lad who had opened his heart to her in the barracks in Paris and whose eyes had met hers as he galloped off after his cat-calling friends?

For a little time after the battle of Rivoli, Pierre had been a hero. It was he who had delivered the order that released Charles Lasalle to hurtle down on the Austrians in the greatest cavalry charge of the campaign. All hussars were heroes on that day. But this one seemed to have lost his mind. All he could talk about was a lady in green, some apparition that had come to him on the battlefield when his lieutenant was injured. Bonaparte himself visited Gaston in hospital, and realising that Gaston would never ride again, had promoted him to captain. Should he survive the infection that was inevitable after his amputation, he would at least have a captain's pension. The deranged cadet was left to dress his wound and see him home if possible.

Gaston took Colette off to see the rest of the chateau and Louise emerged cautiously from behind the curtain. 'Pierre?' she asked, 'Tell me what happened.' He was looking at her, seeing her, she was sure, but his eyes – perhaps his mind – seemed to have lost their ability to focus. She moved closer to him and it was as though a mist had cleared from his vision.

'You're real!' he breathed.

'Yes, Pierre, I am real because you made me real.'

'Am I still mad? If I'm no longer mad, they'll send me back, you know. I don't want that.'

'They won't send you back, Pierre, and you're not mad … you never were.'

'Your dress, it was splashed with blood. I couldn't help it.'

'I don't remember any of it, Pierre. Was I there?'

'Oh yes. It was you who calmed me. Forced me to bind Gaston's leg so he'd lose no more blood. That's when your dress … '

'The dress is not important, Pierre, it isn't marked. What happened then?'

'You stayed with Gaston. You made me take the orders and deliver them to Lasalle. You see, the French line had been broken, in minutes we would all have been swept away. Only the cavalry could stem the tide. I wanted to charge with them, to die with them. I was sure the lieutenant would die and I couldn't bear to be left on my own. Then I remembered that you were waiting beside him, so I returned. I got him across my horse and to a dressing station. When I came out you had gone, so I started looking for you. I asked everyone. They didn't seem to understand.'

Louise and Pierre walked up and down the dining room together as he poured out his story. Neither of them noticed when Gaston and Colette came into the room. It was a wonder that Gaston's roar of delight didn't bring the whole chateau staff running. They stood around her, laughing, wanting to embrace but holding back ...

'Just give me a moment more, Louise,' Gaston laughed. 'I am like poor Brouchard: I see you one minute and then I don't. There, I have you now!' Louise told them how successful they had been in allowing her to see through their eyes, but there were many gaps she wanted filled and they eagerly supplied the details.

Eventually Marie's mother called out that their coach was ready. It was time for them to go.

'But you must come with us, Louise, and where is your picture?' Gaston demanded. 'I promised that I would come back and get you, remember?'

Louise had been preparing herself for this. 'Gaston,' she said. 'It is time for me to move on. You and Colette have each other now. You don't need me. And as for my portrait, don't worry; it is not with the Count. It is in safe hands.'

They did their best to make her change her mind but

deep down they all – except Pierre perhaps – knew that this parting was inevitable. The last goodbyes were said, Gaston and Colette left the room and only Pierre lingered as if unable to move. Louise went up to him, took his hands, and then kissed him on both cheeks.

'You must go too, Pierre. You are safe now, and everything will be all right. I give you my word.'

Jacquot and Marie were to be married in a month. Marie was all for moving straight into the dower house, but Jacquot, for some obscure reason, insisted that they spend the first night of their marriage in his hut. When Marie decided that this was romantic, she entered wholeheartedly into the scheme. It was then that she discovered Louise. It was a tense moment. Jacquot wasn't there; she propped the picture up on the bed and cocked her head to one side.

'The girl in the green dress. I wondered where you'd gone? Now why ...?' Her sharp eyes saw the nearly invisible tear in the canvas. She turned the picture over and looked, suspiciously at first and then appreciatively, at the intricate repair. 'So that's what he was up to. Put a stick through it perhaps and didn't like to confess.' She turned the picture over and curtsied very nicely to Louise; she'd been practising. 'I'm sure you understand, Mademoiselle, but you will just have to find someone else. Jacquot is mine. You will have to go.'

Jean the pedlar and his cart were welcome wherever they traded. As Jacob Abrahams he might not have been so well received; anti-Semitism always lay treacherously just below the surface. He examined Louise's portrait with care, naturally pointing out to Marie that it had been repaired. When Marie told him the price she wanted, a sum so huge that she blushed disarmingly as she named it, she put Jacob in a quandary. He couldn't really bargain up, telling her that it was worth twenty times what she was asking. That wasn't how he worked. He had the grace not to bargain at all and gave the astounded Marie the amount she had asked. As he drove away, with Louise safely packed into his cart, he came to terms with himself. He never said anything to Marie, but it so happened that whenever he passed the little dower house with its growing number of children, he always had some bargain. Some length of priceless silk, or a Sèvres jug, and once even a pretty little spinet that he had 'picked up somewhere for nothing,' and which he could let Marie have for a few sous.

Gaston, Colette, and particularly Pierre, were true to their promises to remember Louise, and, at least in their imaginations, felt her response. For as long as they lived she would share their triumphs and troubles. Colette spent quite a lot of her time in peace negotiations between Lucien and Margot, until to everyone's surprise – and some people's disappointment – Lucien discovered the joys of parenthood. Louise always knew when the grape harvest was in and the first of the juice had begun to flow from the presses. Even now in Les Clos du Bois there is a ceremony when the juice first begins to run. All work stops, glasses are filled and a toast is drunk: *'À la jeune fille en vert!'* Nobody remembers any longer who this mysterious girl in green was, but the toast is drunk with reverence and enthusiasm.

ABOUT *THE RAINBOW BRIDGE*

When I was visiting Amsterdam in search of material for *Wings Over Delft* I had already planned that Louise's portrait would reappear in the hands of a young French hussar at the time of the French Revolution. I had, however, no idea how I would get her portrait to France, let alone into the hands of a hussar. Towards the end of a long day looking at pictures in the Rijksmuseum, I came on a painting in the historical section in the basement of the gallery. I was immediately alert; surely that was a French uniform, and didn't the blue white and red cockade signify the Revolution? The note beside the picture told me that this was a certain General Daendels, a Dutch man who had taken advantage of the frozen Rhine to lead a small French army into the Netherlands. Here he hoped to persuade the City Council in Amsterdam to resign in favour of his French supported Pro-Patriot movement. The date was 1795. I had no idea at the time, of course, what this meant, except that, surely such an army would include a troop of hussars. Already in my mind I could hear the clatter of hooves, and Gaston, dressed in his magnificent uniform, was emerging in my imagination. All I had to do now was to bring Louise's picture and his troop of hussars together.

With a firm date on which to hang my tale, I began to read about that turbulent time and to discover other events that would help to root my story in history. The gruesome details of the Terror, with the march of the guillotine across France, are common knowledge, but the events at Nantes, which Gaston witnesses, are less well known. The uprising of the royalist Vendéeans, their massacre in retreat, and the mass drownings in the Noyades, which Gaston wit-

267

nesses with the port doctor's heartless daughter, still hide in the silence of shame.

It had not been my intention to drag Napoleon into my story just for the sake of the name. But when I discovered that Napoleon was in fact in Paris, looking for work with the Sultan of Turkey, at the time of Gaston's arrival from the Netherlands, I had to think again. Reading on, I found that Napoleon had been a protégé of Robespierre's brother so that, when Robespierre himself was guillotined in 1794, Napoleon came under suspicion, and was in fact in danger of losing his own head. He really had applied to the Sultan for a job, and what would be more likely than that he would recruit one or two likely young officers to serve under him in Turkey? Gaston and his small troop cut a dash when arriving in Paris and could easily have attracted his attention. In later life people who met Napoleon were amazed at how he appeared to know more about them than they knew themselves. His research into Gaston's family would have been in character, as would his examination of the young hussar's abilities. The incident that I recount at the end of the book, at the battle of Lodi, when Napoleon sights the guns himself, has become an icon for Napoleon's relationship with his men. It was here that he was dubbed 'our little corporal' because he was prepared to do a corporal's job to win the day.

In 2000 Jennifer and I went to France and travelled up the Loire, visiting the great chateaux. Then we crossed into the Burgundy area, where fields of wheat alternate with vast tracts of forest, and where deep valleys feed water northwards up into the Seine. The idea of a chateau within the forest came from one that we passed on one of our many walks. When, in search for wine we drove to the village of Irancy, I was immediately entranced by the perfect symmetry of the semicircular valley. The slopes were patterned with the geometric lines of the vines, and I knew that I had found a home for Gaston and an occupation for his family. I had to rely on books to acquire a knowledge of the winemaking process. I was therefore apprehensive, sometime later, when a friend invited us to meet a Frenchman who was an expert on wine. He, however, reminded me so much of my M. Morteau that I ventured to say that I had just been writing about an imaginary winemaker who talked to his grapes and his wines. '*Naturellement*' he said, '*Pourquoi pas?*' I felt that perhaps I had got something right.

A number of books have contributed hugely to my understanding of the time in which *The Rainbow Bridge* is set. Norman Davies's, *Europe A History* not only provided me with a historical framework, but many historical asides as well, such as the story of the 'Marseillaise', and the gruesome details of the Noyades. *The Memoirs of Madame de la Tour du Pin* give a vivid firsthand account of the period. Madame was a member of Marie Antoinette's household who not only survived the Terror but also met and conversed with Napoleon. It is she who records being amazed and disconcerted by Napoleon's knowledge of her family and of her connections, when they met. *A Place of Greater Safety* by Hilary Mantel is a novel, but it gives a good idea of the complex thinking of the leaders of the French Revolution. One of my best sources on the hussars was in fact a children's book, *Hussars of the Napoleonic Wars*, by Kenneth Ulyatt. For light relief I would recommend anyone to read Conan Doyle's *The Adventures of Brigadier Gerard*. After reading this, readers will understand why Napoleon was so anxious to establish that Gaston was not just swagger and bluster. For information on the Napoleonic era I would recommend www.napoleon-series.org.

The Story of Wine by Hugh Johnson is so fascinating that it is difficult to put down. It provided many of the details that went into my descriptions of the Morteau winery. I have the *Encyclopaedia Britannica* on my computer, and use it regularly, often to check the accuracy and reliability of information from Internet sites, which are only as reliable as are the people who have put them up.

Jacquot's surprisingly good education could have put him in the way of the fairy tales of the great French storyteller, Charles Perrault (1628–1703). These stories include *Blue Beard, Little Red Riding Hood,* and *Cinderella.* I have attempted to catch the flavour of Perrault's style in writing Jacquot's tale.

The Louise *trilogy* ...

WINGS OVER DELFT
Book 1: the Louise trilogy

Delft, Holland, 1654. Louise Eeden reluctantly agrees to have her portrait painted. Things are moving too fast in her life. Everyone believes she is engaged to Reynier DeVries; she is chaperoned and protected – a commodity to be exchanged in a marriage that will merge two pottery businesses. In the studio with Master Haitink and his apprentice, Pieter, Louise unexpectedly finds the freedom to be herself. Friendship grows into love, but unknown to Louise, her every move is being reported, and behind the scenes, a web of treachery is gradually unravelling. Then fate, in the form of a careless watchman at the gunpowder store, steps in ...

THE RAINBOW BRIDGE
Book 2

TO COME ...

IN THE CLAWS OF THE EAGLE
Book 3

Vienna, late nineteenth century. Little Isaac Abrahams is showing early signs of talent on the violin. He often practises to an audience of just one – the lady in the picture on the wall of his parents' house. After the Anschluss of 1939, Isaac, now a famous violin virtuoso, is taken to the Theresienstadt concentration camp, and thence to Auschwitz. The portrait of Louise falls into the hands of an SS officer named Heinrich, and seems destined to join the collection being stolen from the galleries and private collection of Europe on the express orders of Adolf Hitler ...